F.A.O. SCHWARZ
TOYS
through the years

1911
1912
1914
1923
1924
1931
1936
1939
1942
1957
1960
1971

Doubleday & Company, Inc.
Garden City, New York

text by Marvin Schwartz
design by Ladislav Svatos

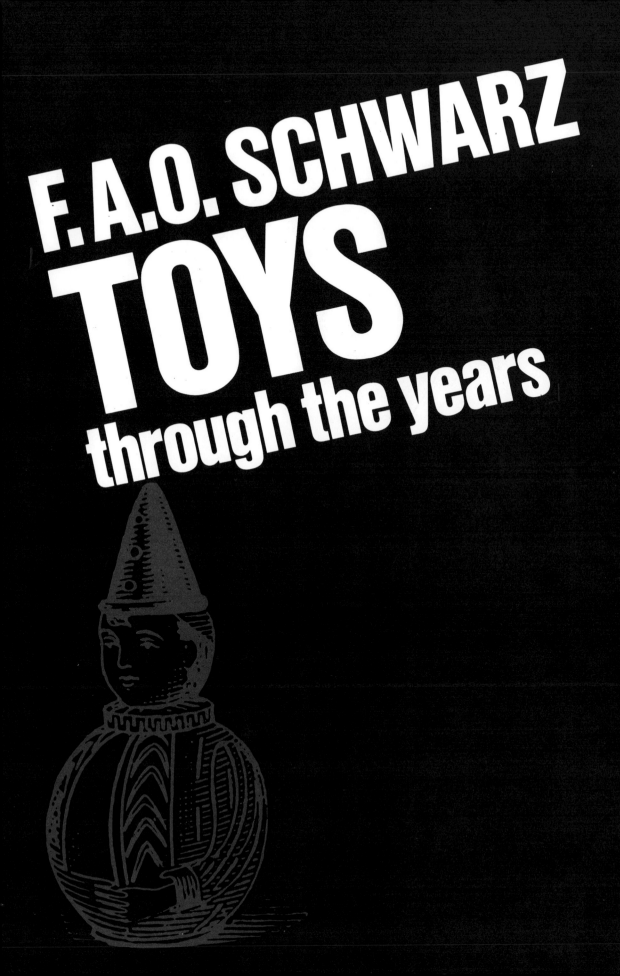

F.A.O. SCHWARZ
TOYS
through the years

ISBN 0-385-07136-1 Trade
0-385-09573-2 Prebound
Library of Congress Catalog Card Number 73–13096

9   8   7   6   5   4   3   2

contents

The illustrations chosen from the F. A. O. Schwarz catalogues were selected as choice examples of the toys children have enjoyed in the past sixty years. Some, like the 1911 tricycle with a full seat and arms for the rider, might seem strange, while others appear modern although they are fifty years old. All are reminders of the fact that children's needs vary only slightly through the years. The sampling includes some of the best of what was available from F. A. O. Schwarz, the country's leading toy retailer. There are low-priced objects as well as those that would be considered expensive, but none of the badly made imitations of fine products that unfortunately are found on the shelves of retailers willing to compromise on quality.

F. A. O. Schwarz opened for business in 1862 at the time toymaking was being transformed from a craft to an important industry. Although toys have been a part of life as long as there have been children, before the 1800s most youngsters had crudely made toys produced at home or by craftsmen who made them cheaply as a sideline. Fine toys were for the very rich and those that have lasted appear to have been made more for show than for play. When toys were manufactured in large quantities at the factories introduced with the Industrial Revolution of the early nineteenth century, a wide range of well-made forms were produced at prices the middle class could afford.

The consistency of the offerings for the sixty years should not be suprising. Even a comparison of ancient examples with their modern counterparts would reveal few differences. Although materials and the way details are drawn have changed with variations in style, toys have always been the tools children use to act out their fantasies about adult life. Many are simply scale models of objects used for ordinary (or extraordinary) daily activities. Small furniture, machines, wagons or cars have been devices children use to mimic their elders. For the make-believe world, extra friends in the form of dolls were the exclusive domain of girls. When the baby doll was introduced about 1850, it was part of the group of child dolls that provided pretend families for make-believe mothers, and adult dolls were all but forgotten. Recently, adult dolls have regained popularity and boys and girls both have "special" grown-up friends.

Toys are reserved for acting out scenes from everyday life while games are an aspect of play that involves the child in the struggles of life. Games make competition possible on terms that are pleasant because, hopefully, nobody goes away angry. Some games are tests of physical ability, such as sports like baseball or football. Chess and checkers are battles of the intellect, while in card games and dice, chance is a major factor that may be exploited best by a degree of thinking that differs from game to game.

For ancient man, sports were religious ceremonies. The Olympics of Ancient Greece were a part of the Festival honoring the King of the Greek Gods, Zeus. While today, there is no religious significance to football competitions, the passions aroused are as fervent. Fewer and fewer adults play football or baseball. They prefer watching professionals. Children, on the other hand, have a good time competing at these sports and proud parents provide proper equipment so the small-sized football and baseball uniforms have been in the Schwarz catalogues for years.

As you look over the toys and games that have been offered by F. A. O. Schwarz, you will see how they can serve as a barometer of fashion. Dolls more often wear fashionable outfits; cars of the early years were very much like the latest on the road. Warships were more popular during the threat of war or in wartime than in a period of peace. Toys and games remind us of the wonderful years of play and the changes they document are evidence of how the world evolves.

Dolls

Dolls representing adult soldiers, doctors, firemen or athletes help children act out their ambitions for adulthood but in the years between the 1860s and 1950s they were very rare. During that period, dolls were made almost exclusively for girls. Recently there has been a revival of adult dolls so that you can now find an example representing an athlete or a soldier that affords a boy the same opportunity to act out his dreams as the pretty teen-ager doll affords the girl who can make believe she is at last old enough to wear make-up and have her hair done. Dolls had reflected the popular conception of the differences between boys and girls, which had boys scooting around with their footballs, archery sets and dump trucks, building, fighting and being generally active while the girls were expected to concentrate on matters around the house. Ideas had begun to change in the late 1940s when women joined the army and were working in defense factories, but it was not until the 1950s that boys had dolls for their own use once more.

The dolls of the early 1900s are elegantly dressed in fairly formal clothing. They appear in sailor outfits because these were summer clothes for girls and boys that were the closest to casual dress allowed by substantial middle-class families. Otherwise, frills were required in the days when no one dreamed of wearing jeans or overalls. You can see skirt lengths rise as time goes on but otherwise elegantly dressed girl dolls were standard until the 1940s. Nurses uniforms, ballet outfits and riding clothes were sometimes worn by dolls that were provided with more than one outfit. By the 1960s, Charles Addams dolls were introduced as children relaxed and joked more about dolls as well as the scary world of ghosts. Doll carriages suggest the spirit of manners of each decade. In 1911 the baby sat in a carriage that was so slick it could have been used in a parade. Even in 1931 the bassinet and cradle looked as if they were set for a state viewing rather than for practical baby care, but by the 1940s the more functional Bathinette was provided in the appropriate size for dolls.

Size	6 in.	7 in.	8 in.	9 in.	10 in.
Price	60c.	70c.	80c.	90c.	$1.00

10½ in.	13 in. Pa-Ma	14 in.	18 in.
25c.	50c.	50c.	$1.00

French Jointed Dolls — (Special Bargain.)

With bisque head, long hair, shoes and stockings, at very attractive prices

(No shoes and stockings)

Size,	10½ in.	14 in.	18 in.		Moving	10½ in.	13 in.	17 in.
Price,	25c.	50c.	$1.00		eyes,	30c.	50c.	$1.00

Fine French Full Jointed Dolls.

In shirt, with shoes and stockings, moving eyes, curly hair, jointed wrists.

Size	14 in.	17 in.	20 in.	24 in.	27 in.
Price	$1.00	$1.50	$2.00	$3.00	$4.00

Fine French Full Jointed Dolls with Perfect Baby Face

Short hair wig, moving eyes, in long baby shirt.

Size	11 in.	13 in.	17 in.	21 in.	23 in.
Price	$1.00	$1.50	$2.25	$3.75	$3.50

No. 1340. Heavy white linen blouse suit. Pleated skirt, tan Shantung box coat, large white chip hat. Boy dressed to match.

BOY		GIRL	
13 in.........$ 5.00		13 in..........$ 6.00	
15 in......... 6.00		15 in.......... 7.00	
17 in..... 8.00		17 in......... 9.00	
20 in.......... 10.00		20 in......... 11.00	

No. 1324. White net dress, trimmed with heavy white lace, bias fold at bottom of skirt of pink or blue silk. Same color tucked belt and shoulder straps. White straw bonnet with ribbon trimming.

8½ in. **$2.25,** 11 in. **3.50,** 13 in. **5.00** 17 in. **8.00,** 22 in. **12.00**

No. 1323. Pink or blue silk dress, lace trimmed. Black sash. Neapolitan straw hat of black, trimmed with pink moss-rose buds and ribbon.

15 in....$6.00		17 in....$8.00	
20 in....10.00		22 in....12.00	

No. 1341. Pink or blue silk dress, shirred at waist, tucked skirt, trimmed with lace. Fichu of silk forms waist trimming. Straw bonnet of white with frills of white lace

13 in....$5.00		15 in....$6.00	
17 in.... 7.50		22 in.....12.00	

No. 1300. Gray and black hair stripe silk dress, bias fold of black silk at bottom of skirt piped with red. Buttons of same color. Black straw bonnet, red ribbon trimmed.

13 in... $6.00		15 in....$6.50	
17 in.... 8.50		20 in....11.00	
22 in.................13.50			

"THE LUXURY"
With large Storm Apron

"**Luxury,**" body 37x18 inches, dark green, maroon and dark blue finish, plain cycle wheels 16x22 inches, ⅝-inch rubber tires and brake........**$35.00**

Furnished with nickel-plated tangent spoke wheels 16x22 inches, ⅝-inch rubber tires and nickel trimmings throughout, and brake 40.00

Hair Mattress to fit............................ 3.75

Bodies finished in White Enamel, $5.00 extra

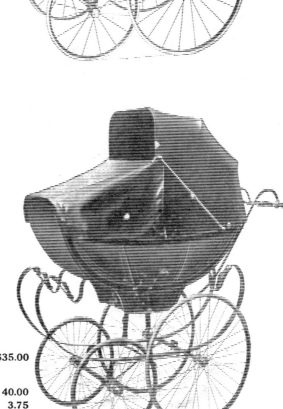

"ENGLISH MAIL CART"

No. 3701. Full size body, same high finish as S/14. Wheels 12x22 in., ⅝-inch rubber tires.

Price..........................**$40.00**

White finish, **$5.00** extra

"THE BABY BOAT"
With large Storm Apron

"**Baby Boat,**" body 37x18 inches, dark green, maroon and dark blue finish, plain cycle wheels 16x22 inches, ⅝-inch rubber tires and brake....**$35.00**

Furnished with nickel-plated tangent spoke wheels 16x22 inches, ⅝-inch rubber tires and nickel trimmings throughout and brake.... .... 40.00

Hair Mattress to fit............................ 3.75

Bodies finished in White Enamel $5.00 extra

No. 418. PULLMAN SLEEPER
Price, $42.00

Body. White Enamel.
Upholstering. White Fine Corduroy with Box Cushion.
Sliding Hood. Reed, White. Upholstered like Body. Removable Back Curtain. Nickel Plated Adjustment.
Gear. Steel Tubular Turntable, Four 16-inch Cushion Artillery Rubber Tire Wheels. Patent Anti-Friction Wheel Fastener. Foot Brake. Enamel Finish. Enameled Push Bar.

No. 411. PULLMAN SLEEPER
Price, $32.00

Body. Wood, with Reed Roll, painted Brown with Ecru Fibre Panels, Varnished.
Upholstering. Pongee Corduroy with Mattress Cushion.
Sliding Hood. Reed, painted Brown, Varnished. Upholstered like Body. Removable Back Curtain. Nickel Plated Adjustment.
Gear. Steel Tubular Turntable, Four 16 x ½-inch Artillery Rubber Tire Wheels. Patent Anti-Friction Wheel Fastener. Foot Brake. Enamel Finish. Enameled Push Bar.

No. E 45. STATIONARY GO-CART
Price, $15.00

Body. Reed, Varnished.
Gear. Steel Tubular, 12 x 16 x ½-inch Rubber Tire Wheels. Patent Anti-Friction Wheel Fastener. Foot Brake. Enamel Finish. Enameled Push Bar.
White Enamel Finish, **$2.50** extra.

RED RIDING HOOD DOLL

No. RH/34 — Blue gingham dress, white dimity apron, red cotton cape with hood, size of doll 13 inches ....$ 7.50
No. RH/39—Same, but 16 in. 8.50
No. RHS/34—Blue silk dress, white silk apron, trimmed with lace, red silk cape, lined with white, size of doll 13 inches 10.00
No. RHS/39—Same, but 16 in. 12.00

No. 560—White lawn dress with pink or blue collar and cuffs, edged with lace, brocaded corduroy coat and hat, doll 20 inches $15.00
22 inches 18.00
29 inches 30.00

BABY DOLLS
(Short Dress)

Fine short white dress with two rows of tucks on bottom of skirt, square yoke with tucks, trimmed with insertion, lace and ribbons in pink or blue, cap to match.
No. 1235/28 Baby Doll, 11 inches ....$ 6.00
No. 1235/32 Baby Doll, 13 inches 7.00
No. 1235/36 Baby Doll, 15 inches 8.00
No. 1235/42 Baby Doll, 16½ inches 10.00
No. 1235/50 Baby Doll, 20 inches 12.00
Large sizes, in finer dresses, ranging from
....$24.00 to $30.00

WALKING DOLL

No. 196—Will walk, when led by hand (not mechanical) and move head left and right. Doll is of the same quality as our "Favorite" Doll on page 4. White organdy dress with pink and blue organdy collar and cuffs, and fold on bottom of skirt, edged with lace doll 20 inches $14.00
25 inches 20.00

HAT BOX

No. 2/32/2—Red box 8 inch diameter, with 6 inch bisque head girl doll, sleeping eyes, 2 dresses with underwear, hat, bag, mirror and brush $4.75

No.2/32/4—Red Box 8¾ inch diameter, with 7½ inch bisque head baby doll, 2 dresses, coat, hat, worsted jacket and cap, bottle............... 6.00

"KAETHE KRUSE" DOLLS

In addition to the illustrated dolls (Matten and Kathrinchen) we carry in stock a variety of about 30 different styles, prices ranging according to dress:

Series A—Boys or Girls, plain dressés, 16 in., painted hair....$13.50
Series B—Boys or Girls, better dresses 15.00
Series C—Boys or Girls, fine dresses 16.50
Series D—Boys or Girls, best dresses 18.00
Undressed—Doll with combination 10.00

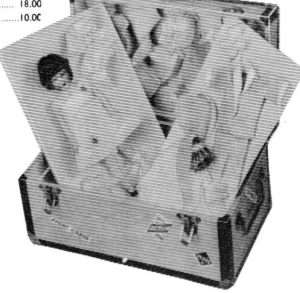

TROUSSEAU TRUNK

No. 25/12/1—Trunk 11 inch with tray, 8½ inch girl doll with bisque head, 2 dresses, coat and hat, pajamas, bag and apron $7.50
No. 25/12/2—Same as above, but larger 10.00

BASSINETTE ON WHEELS

No. 305—Inside length 23 inches, finish ivory, height 27 inches, trimmed with ribbon and lace. Mattress with pillow, 2 sheets, pillow case, blanket, spread and sham $20.00

No. 146—Body 25x13 inches with foot extension, fully upholstered, painted wheels, rubber tires, handlebar 28 inches high, handbrake, colors dark blue or cream with nile $16.50

CRADLE

No. 61—Cretonne covered, small flower design, inside length 14 inches $5.75
No. 60—Same, but 10 inches long   3.00

PATSY BABYKIN

No. A-3721—We take pleasure in announcing the arrival of this cute new baby in the Patsy family. She's just opening her eyes. How adorable—life-like as can be. She lies down and turns her head to look at you. She sits up, too, straight as a two-year old. Her arms move, her legs move—she takes the most cunning positions. Of almost unbreakable composition with movable eyes, head and limbs. About 10" high..$1.85
No. A-3722—Doll including pillow and ribbon.... 2.25
No. A-3701—This is Patsy Babykin, too, but this time she wears the cutest short, curly hair of soft baby lambskin—so it really washes. She is made just like her sister of almost unbreakable composition, with movable eyes, head and limbs. 10" high. **Mention color of wig**...............................$3.00

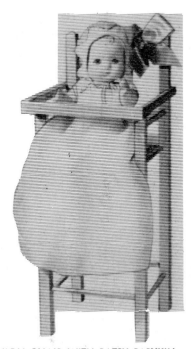

HIGH CHAIR WITH PATSY BABYKIN

No. A-0399—Patsy Babykin has high chair of her very own painted in ivory and tied with a big pink or blue bow. The chair, 18" high, has a tray which can be raised out of the way and a footrest. Patsy Baby has a long white organdy dress bound with pink or blue at the neck and featherstitched in front. Her slip is lace trimmed. State color of bow. Complete $4.50
Chair, separately 1.00

THE TWINS (PATSY BABYKINS)

No. A-3752—What little girl in all the world doesn't adore twins, especially when they're Patsy Baby-kins? Each has a baby-bunting of fine flannel—one pink and one blue. There is a dainty dotted swiss cover for the pillow top; the twins and all are wrapped in a soft, ribbon bound blanket with bow in pink. The dolls are the regular Patsy Babies with almost unbreakable composition bodies, movable eyes, head and limbs. 10" high. Complete........$5.00

PLAY YARD WITH PATSY BABYKIN

No. A-0400—Room enough for Patsy Babykin to play around in her own yard. It is nicely made of wood, ivory colored, with either pink or blue figured blanket and ribbon bows. Yard is 13½" square and the rail is 5¾" high. There is a lovely iridescent, floating swan, Patsy Baby's own toilet set and talc, soap, towel, face-cloth and hot water bottle. Patsy Babykin is the darling 10" doll with sleeping eyes and movable head and limbs. She, **our own creation**, has a rattle. State color. Complete..........$5.00
Play yard, separately, untrimmed........................ 1.25

Dressed Dolls.

French Full Jointed Dolls, finer quality, dressed in the latest styles.

irls—$2.50, $2.75, $3.50, $3.75, $4.00, $4.50, $5.00, $5.50, $6.00, $6 50, $7.00, $8.00,
$8.50 $9.00, $10 00, $12.00, $13.50, $14.00, $15.00, $18.00, $22 00, $28.00, $30.

oys..............................$2.00, $2.25, $2.50, $3.50, $4.00, $4.50, $5.00, $5.50, $6.

Bisque Jointed Dolls.

Small, in fancy costumes, from 12c. to $1.25.

Dressed Dolls, suitable for Doll Houses.

In all the different costumes, as Housekeepers, Ladies, Gentlemen, Children, Nurses,
Waiters, Cooks, Coachmen, etc.

oll Heads, bisque, with moving eyes, and long hair (see cut), $1.00, $1.25,
$1.50, $1.75, $2.00, $2.25, $2.50, $3.

oll Bodies, muslin, with kid arms and hands, shoes and stockings, best
quality, 9 sizes, from 10 in. to 18 in., 50c. to $3.

oll Bodies, kid jointed, with jointed arms, 90c., $1.00, $1.25, $1.50, $1.75,

No. 25/155—Princess Elizabeth—Here is a princess for a playmate—a dream come true. Her jointed composition body measures 16" tall. Her moving eyes have real lashes and her blonde curls are real hair. She wears a long white evening dress with a silk slip, a red velvet cape with ermine tails, carries a white evening bag, and her slippers are silver............**$5.75**

No. 25/150—Princess Elizabeth—In a larger size, 20"......................**$7.50**

Wendy Ann Doll—Like the human body, this Doll with its extra joint can bend at the thigh as well as at the waist. The result is a surprisingly flexible body developing more natural and graceful positions with easier dressing, etc. She has pretty features, hands and limbs, sleeping eyes, curly hair and measures 13½" tall.

No. 25/147—Navy blue fall coat and hat over light blue dress with darker blue trim.........**$4.00**

No. 25/146—Flowered cotton dress with white bodice and bonnet **3.00**

No. 25/148—Full Riding Habit............. **3.00**

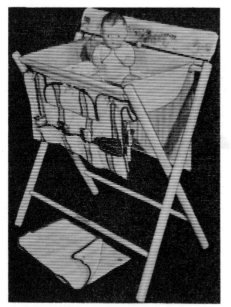

No. 6 – 1—Bathinette—A perfect miniature reproduction of a real baby's bathinette. Built on strong wooden frame, 17 x 16 x 11". It's enameled in a soft ivory shade. The rubber tube has a drain to let the water run out. Over the top is a white canvas cover which turns the bathinette into a handy table when bathing time is over. The bathinette is trimmed with figured sateen. A terry cloth bag has pockets which hold powder, soap, sponge, face cloth and towel with rubber sheeting. Baby doll is 11" tall, made of rubber so she really can be washed, and has a turnable head. She's wearing a romper. TRIMMED IN OUR STUDIO. **$6.75**

Doll's Wardrobe Trunk—When dolly must a-journeying go, wouldn't it be nice to have a roomy trunk to pack her clothes in! Metal covered in blue, all decorated with steamship pasters, like a real traveller's. Strongly made with metal bracing, shiny brass corners, lock and fittings Attractively finished inside.

No. 9 – 34—With 3 drawers, 9 x 9 x 16". **$3.00**
No. 9 – 35—With 4 drawers, 9¾ x 11 x 18". **3.75**
No. 6 – 58—A better grade with 3 wooden drawers, 11 x 11½ x 20". **5.75**
No. 6 – 38—As above but with 4 good size wooden drawers on one side and a shoe drawer on the other. Size 12 x 12 x 24". **$9.50**

No. 9 – 47—Double Decker Bed—Designed to save space without losing comfort, the idea has appealed to many children for their own use so why not for their dolls as well? Made of wood, maple finish, measuring 14 x 27 x 24" high. Complete with ladder to reach upper bed. Each bed fitted with mattress, pillow, sheets, and blanket. Covered with a figured organdy spread lined with pink or blue sateen. STATE COLOR.
OUR OWN TRIMMING. **$16.75**

26-32 CISSY IN BRIDAL GOWN Ship. wt. 7 lbs. **25.00**
ite tulle gown has pleated skirt, lace bodice and
n sash pulled through loop of pearls. Medici cap
chapel length veil. Bridal bouquet, pearl necklace
ring.

C 26-25 CISSY AS QUEEN ELIZABETH **25.00**
Court gown of white brocade, worn over taffeta hoop
petticoat, with sash of the Garter with star, long
white gloves, and tiara, earrings and bracelets jeweled with rhinestones. Ship. wt. 7 lbs.

D 26-15 CISSY IN COCKTAIL DRESS
Ship. wt. 7 lbs. **17.95**
Smart blue taffeta long torso dress,
worn over can-can petticoat. Separate
velvet bolero, tiny veiled hat of
flowers, rhinestone bracelet and afternoon bag.

E 26-9 CISSY IN AFTERNOON DRESS
Ship. wt. 7 lbs. **17.95**
Stylish red dotted Swiss organdy dress
worn over white taffeta can-can petticoat that rustles when she walks.
Smart veiled straw hat trimmed with
flowers. Hatbox included.

1957

A KATHY BABY Sweet-faced little charmer, made entirely of soft molded vinyl and fully jointed for versatile play. Kathy has rooted Saran hair, goes to sleep, cries real tears, has a voice, drinks and wets. She, is dressed in lace-trimmed organdy with frothy bonnet of shirred lace ruffles. Satin baby shoes complete her costume.

16-20 15" tall. Ship. wt. 3 lbs. **10.95**
26-12 19" tall. Ship. wt. 4 lbs. **13.95**
16-19 21" tall. Ship. wt. 5 lbs. **18.95**

ELISE, the Sweet Sixteen Doll — Having just outgrown her tomboy days, Elise's pretty face mirrors the wide-eyed innocence of her tender age. 16" tall (and just that age, too) she is brand new from the top of her Saran hair to the tip of her graceful toes. She walks, sits and kneels, and with her jointed ankles can wear high or low heels. Her shapely body and head (with moving eyes) are of hard plastic and her jointed arms of soft vinyl. Ship. wt. 3 lbs. each.

B 26-82 ELISE IN COAT AND HAT **12.95**
Chocolate brown velvet coat, lined with pink taffeta, covers pink taffeta dress, and has matching hat.

C 26-84 ELISE IN BALLERINA COSTUME **11.95**
Over her long pink tights, Elise wears a nylon tulle tou-tou attached to blossom-trimmed satin bodice, and satin ballet slippers.

D 26-13 ELISE IN AFTERNOON DRESS......................**10.95**
Pink checked taffeta dress with lace-trimmed nylon puff sleeves and flower-trimmed hat.

Size	6 in.	7 in.	8 in.	8½ in.	9 in.
Price	30c.	35c.	40c.	45c.	50c.

DOLL'S REPAIRING DEPARTME

pairing is in the most skillful hands and promptly
Jointed Dolls restrung.
New Heads, Arms, Legs, Wigs supplied.
Real Hair Wigs made to order.

Dolls' Trousseaux in Trunks, very complete, **$3.00, $3.75,**
$5.00. (see cut), $6.75 $8.50, $9.00, $10.00, $15.00, $20.00, $30.00
Dolls' Trousseaux in Baskets, $2.00, $2.75, $6.00, $8.50
Dolls' Toilet Boxes and Baskets, furnished complete, 25c. to $18.0
Dolls' Jewelry Sets, many new kinds ....10c. to $4.5
Also Dolls' Dresses, Hats, Caps, Shoes, Stockings, Parasols, etc., etc., in very large variety.

RAGGEDY ANN AND ANDY (All ages)—Famous brother and sister story book characters make gay playmates. Both are stuffed with cotton, have red cotton yarn hair, painted features with shoe button eyes and are authentically dressed. Books not included.

819-99 RAGGEDY ANN 24" tall. 3 lbs. **5.95**
819-100 RAGGEDY ANDY 24" tall. 3 lbs. **5.95**
819-103 RAGGEDY ANN 30" tall. 4 lbs. **8.95**
819-101 RAGGEDY ANDY 30" tall. 4 lbs. **8.95**
840-254 RAGGEDY ANN 48" tall. Express . . . **30.00**
Ship wt. 11 lbs.
840-257 RAGGEDY ANDY 48" tall. Express . . . **30.00**
Ship. wt. 11 lbs.
856-50 RAGGEDY ANN STORIES BOOK **2.50**
856-51 RAGGEDY ANDY STORIES BOOK ... **2.50**

CHARLES ADDAMS DOLLS—Designed after the eerie but oddly appealing characters in Charles Addams's cartoons are these three stuffed dolls. All are dressed faithfully to their cartoon appearance in cotton clothes of appropriate design and color. Ship. wt. 4 lbs. ea.

826-115 WEDNESDAY 20" tall........**7.95**
826-157 WEDNESDAY'S MOTHER
MORTICIA 45" tall **19.95**
826-156 IRVING 20" tall **7.95**

G 815-186 SPRING DOLL Ship. wt. 2 lbs. 6.95
The heroine of "Spring Is A New Beginning" (see below), is a 13" doll with
soft body covered by her organdy-trimmed yellow dress.
857-007 "SPRING IS A NEW BEGINNING" BOOK 1.95
A lovely little book that captures the joy of springtime.

H 816-073 LOVE DOLL Ship. wt. 2 lbs. 6.95
Out of the pages of "Love Is A Special Way of Feeling" (see below), she is a soft-
bodied 12" doll in a cotton dress with lace-trimmed apron.
857-008 "LOVE IS A SPECIAL WAY OF FEELING" BOOK 1.95
A heart-warming description of happiness charmingly illustrated.

J 816-067 BRAVE COWBOY DOLL Ship. wt. 2 lbs. 7.95
Every inch the western hero, to the top of his flat-crown cowboy hat. 16" tall,
soft, with cloth face, he wears denim pants, felt boots, holsters (with six-shooters),
white shirt, red bandana, gloves and a fearless air.
857-006 "BRAVE COWBOY" BOOK 2.25
857-016 "COWBOY AND FRIENDS" BOOK 2.25
857-014 "COWBOY'S SECRET LIFE" BOOK 2.25
(3 to 7 yrs.)—About a small boy and his imaginary playmates.

K 816-066 THE GIRL DOLL Ship. wt. 2 lbs. 6.95
This red-haired girl stepped right out of the pages of "A Friend Is Someone
Who Likes You," (see below) with her long white stockings, pantaloons, print
dress and white pinafore. 12" tall, soft cloth face.
857-020 "A FRIEND IS SOMEONE WHO LIKES YOU" BOOK 1.95
(3 to 7 yrs.)—Adults and teen-agers have found the small pictures of children and
the happy story most endearing.

Things with wheels

Wheels for children are either practical transportation or, more poetically, vehicles for imaginative trips into the world of play. The small bicycles of 1911, intended primarily as a means of getting somewhere, were neither different from the larger versions nor modern ones, although they lacked the gears now a standard accessory. The tricycles and velocipedes of 1911 are more distinctive. The elaborate seat with arms on one model demanded a more sedate and stately position than any five-year-old of the 1970s could tolerate.

Automobile travel has changed since 1912 for young people as well as their elders. At that time, a ride in an open car necessitated the wearing of a duster to protect good clothing and special goggles and caps. F. A. O. Schwarz offered the proper accessories with their small cars. In both model and toy cars they kept up with changing designs. The 1926 farm wagon is unexpected since it is easy to forget that while the motor car was taking over the roads, horses were still an important source of power on farms. The suggestion that a goat could be harnessed to the wagon reminds us that farm animals were more readily available then than now.

Steam engines were also common in the late 1920s for bright children who might harness the power generated to a variety of machines. The engines also moved wheels and could be used to pull another vehicle. There is little interest in steam today since gasoline and battery driven motors are more likely sources of power. It is amusing to remember that a device such as the steam engine, used first in the eighteenth century, and still significant in the 1920s and 1930s, is now out-of-date. Model cars and dump trucks have been popular toys for the beach and back yard for years. Trucks of the 1920s and earlier vary only slightly from recently made examples. Toy and model automobiles, however, have been all but replaced by racers, since children prefer speed in their play to ordinary drives in the family car.

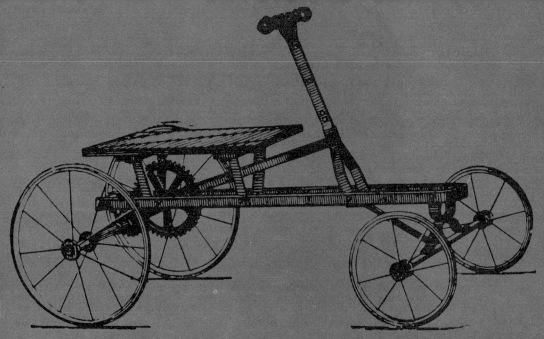

PLAIN BEARING KEYSTONE HAND CAR

Steel frames, 1½ inch rubber tires, wood seat.

No. 116. 29 inches over all, wheels 7x9 inches...............$3.75

No. 119. 36 inches over all, wheels 8x12 inches............. 4.50

No. 213. **Tandem Hand Car,** wheels 8x12 inches, 55 inches over all.. 7.50

Velocipedes.

No. 1,	Front wheel 16 in.,	hind wheels 12 in.............	$2 00
" 2,	" " 20 "	" " 12 ".............	2 50
" 3,	" " 24 "	" " 16 ".............	3 00
" 4,	" " 2 "	" " 16 ".............	3 50

JUVENILE SPALDINGS' BICYCLES

Main frame tubes 1 inch, flush joints. Seat post cluster of new design with binding bolt; fork crown, drop forged, with diamond top. Finished in black enamel with red head, rims to match. 1⅜ in. single tube Fiske tires. Gear 64. Chain 3/16 in. Rubber Pedals. Padded Saddles. Upcurved adjustable handlebar.

FOR BOYS		FOR GIRLS	
14 in. frame	...........$20.00	14 in. frame	...........$20.00
16 in. frame	.... 22.50	16 in. frame	.... 22.50
18 in. frame	.... 25.00	18 in. frame	.... 25.00

Coaster Brakes $5.00 extra

PLAIN BEARING VELOCIPEDE

Best and strongest made. Frames finished in bright maroon enamel. Wheels have ⅝ in. rubber tires, leather saddle seat, adjustable handle bar. When ordering please state leg measure.

"FAIRY" BALL-BEARING TRICYCLES

Frames made of Bicycle Tubing, enameled in Maroon, Nickel-plated Spokes.
WITH CUSHION TIRES

Front wheel 10 in., hind wheels 18 in., for girls under 4 years $12.00
Front wheel 14 in., hind wheels 24 in., for girls from 4 to 6 years................ 15.00
Front wheel 14 in., hind wheels 28 in., for girls from 6 to 10 years.............. .... 18.00
When ordering please state Leg Measure.

"FAIRY" BALL-BEARING AUTO-COASTERS

The most modern Hand Car yet offered, equipped with hand brake, clutch to release gear wheel to permit coasting.
Beautiful design and finish. Made in two sizes, wheels of both 10x14 in.
Frame of small car 32 in. long.... ....Price **$22.00**
Frame of large car 36 in. long...Price **22.50**

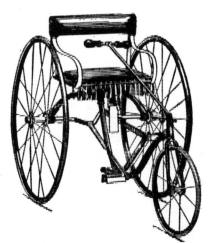

PLAIN BEARING TRICYCLE

Best and strongest made. Frames finished in bright maroon enamel. Wheels have ½ in. rubber tires, seat upholstered with imitation leather. When ordering please state leg measure.

No.	Front Wheel	Rear Wheels	For Child of	Price
60	10 inches	18 inches	3 to 5	**$6.75**
61	12 inches	20 inches	4 to 6	**8.00**
62	12 inches	24 inches	6 to 10	**9.50**
63	14 inches	28 inches	10 to 12	**11.00**

No. 909. PLAIN BEARINGS

Body 11x28, made of sheet steel and wood; painted chrome yellow, with fernleaf green radiator; front striped with gold bronze. Gear enameled black. Wheels, 8-inch and 12-inch, ½-inch R. T., enameled red. Suitable for very small children. Including 2 Lamps and Horn. Price...$10.00

AUTOMOBILE CAPS
Assorted sizes...........65c., $1.25

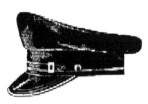

BRASS AUTOMOBILE HORNS

No.	**1.**	Straight horn, brass........................	**$ .50**
No.	**2.**	(See cut) larger and curved....................	**1.00**
No.	**17.**	Horns with long tube.........................	**2.25**

SEARCH LIGHT
Polished brass, to burn oil, each $1.25

MOHAWK. Plain Bearings
Body, 14½x41½, made of sheet steel and wood; painted chrome green outside, red inside, and red radiator front; striped with white and gold bronze. Fenders and foot board enameled black. Gear enameled black. Wheels, 10-inch and 16-inch, ½-inch R. T., enameled red, with brass-plated hub caps. Cushion seat. Suitable for children from 6 to 9 years. Including 2 Lamps and Horn. Price....................... $18 00

Automobile Goggles......20c.

39

1923

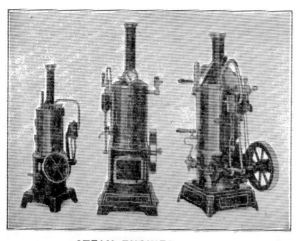

STEAM ENGINES

With fine brass boiler (steel blue) and steam whistle:

No. 322/1½—11 inches high $3.00
No. 322/3—12½ inches high 5.00
No. 322/5—15 inches high 10.00

A finer grade with more details, such as water-gauge, etc.

No. 354/2—15 in., $12.00; No. 354/4—16½
in. 20.00

Very fine engines, with reverse action, governor, manometer, water-gauge, self-oiler, etc.

No. 359/2—13¾ inches 25.00
No. 359/4—15¾ inches 40.00

LOCOMOBILES

Driven by steam, can be used as stationary engine by disconnecting chain, with water-gauge and attachment to shut off steam, etc. Made in 2 sizes:

No. 502/3— 8 in. long, 11½ in. high $12.00
No. 502/5—12 in. long, 16¾ in. high 22.50

STEAM ROLLERS

Run by steam forward or backward.

No. 10/119/0—7 inches long, 6 inches high $5.00
No. 10/119/1—9 inches long, 6¼ inches high 7.50

STATIONARY LOCOMOBILES

Very beautiful engines with innumerable little details, style like above illustration, but without wheels, mounted on a base.

No. 512/2—14½ inches long, 10 inches high $35.00
No. 512/3—17 inches long, 12 inches high 55.00

ATTACHMENTS

Large variety, made of metal, beautifully painted, such as:

Fountains, pumps, windmills, dredges, ferris-wheels, sawmills, from ....$2.00 to $5.00

Gas Motor.

**Of 1-32 Horse Power. Height, 10 in. Length, about 14 in.
Diameter of fly-wheel, 8 in.
Manipulation very simple. Small consumption of gas.**

Price $32.00

No. 107.
4 SIZES.
$4.50, $6.50, $10.00, $15 00

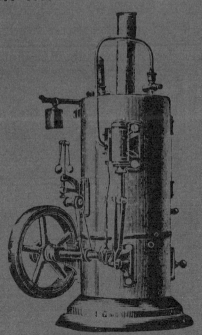

No. 100.
3 SIZES.
$45.00, $60.00, $80.00

1924

PEDI-CAR

Pedi-Car, the highest grade vehicle of this type, has ball-bearing bicycle pedals, nickel-plated handlebar with rubber bike grips, wooden seat, ball-bearing wheels with one inch tires, front wheel 10 inches, rear 8 inches.................................. $10.00

SKATEMOBILE

"Original"—30 inches long. Seat can be laid down to allow rider to stand up. With brake and bell $6.75

Disc Wheel "Pedi-Cycle" with a regular motorbike stand, finished in red. Wheels 11 inch with one inch rubber tire **$6.75**

KIDDIE KARS

With rubber-tired disc wheels, for inside use, an additional improvement to the famous original "Kiddie Kar." Made in 3 sizes $3.00, $3.75, $4.50

Kiddie Kar, with wooden wheels, in 3 sizes $2.00, $2.50, 2.75

RICKENBACKER

"Rickenbacker." Finished in red. Length 52 inches, 12 x ¾ inch rubber-tired disc wheels, roller bearing...............................$35.00

JEWETT

"Jewett." Finished in red. Length 52 inches, 10 x ½ inch rubber-tired disc wheels, roller bearing...............................$30.00

FIRE ENGINE

No. 5586—"Fire Engine." Finished in bright red, with yellow s t r i p i n g. Equipped with nickel-plated boiler 11 x 25 inches, steam gauge, fire door, fire bell, road lamps, spot light. Body 13 x 45 inches, wheels 12 inch ball bearing disc steel, with ⅝ inch rubber tires. For children five to eight years.............$40.00

HOOK AND LADDER

No. 5584—Hook and Ladder.. Body 13 x 56 inches; painted bright red, striped in lemon yellow, nickel-plated trimmings, upholstered seat, extension ladders, bell, lantern, s-t-a-r-t-i-n-g crank bumper, equipped with ¾ inch solid rubber tires and disc wheels............................$40.00

FARM WAGON

A typical farm wagon with red body and seat, varnished wheels and gear. The sides and end are detachable, shaved spokes and welded tires. Body measures 18 x 36 inches, wheels 15 and 21 inches ....each $15.00
Shaft for goats, dogs, etc., to match above wagon 4.50
Harness, leather, adjustable.................$6.00; 10.00

BUDDY "L" DUMP BODY TRUCK

25 inches long, has practical hoisting and unloading device with locking ratchet, disc wheels, painted in red. Chassis and construction entirely of steel, incl. set of rubber tires. Fine for use with the steam shovel $7.50
Hydraulic Dump Truck. Truck body is raised by hydraulic power", after a lever on the side is released. The latest construction, otherwise like above 8.50

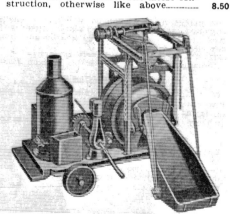

BUDDY "L" CONCRETE MIXER

Sand and cement goes in the big scoop, as it rests on the ground. Turning the crank, the scoop raises by itself and pours the sand, cement and water (coming from the tank) right into the drum, which mixes it all up inside. The finished concrete runs out of a little trough. 16 in. long, 15 in. high, 13 in. wide $13.50

BUDDY "L" FIRE ENGINE

A companion toy for the Buddy "L" Fire Truck. Painted in the same Fire Department red with a nickeled boiler. Has brass hand rails for those riding on the rear step. Length 25 inches $12.00

BUDDY "L" SAND LOADER

Stands 20 inches high; has 12 buckets mounted on two chains, lowering and raising attachment on strong, substantial base. Painted in grey baked-on enamel $10.00

BUDDY "L" RAILWAY EXPRESS TRUCK

26 inches long, with green body, incl. set of rubber tires $8.50

Buddy "L" Small Derrick, a practical operating derrick with windlass for raising and lowering boom. Height 21 inches, base 10 inches square $6.00
Large Derrick, with grab bucket 12.00

YOUTHS' BICYCLES

Youth's Olympic—A special feature in the youth's models is the drop bar, which lowers the saddle two inches, thus giving the rider the advantages of the larger frame and wheels. Colors: Red with black head and stripings, rims and mud guards enameled to correspond.

AJ11—Frame equal to regular 17-inch; wheels 26 inches (for ages from 8 to 10 years) $35.00

A67—Frame equal to regular 19-inch; wheels 28 inches 38.50

BOYS' BICYCLES

Boy's Special—To meet the special requirements of small boys, we have built a bicycle which embodies all the features necessary to make it suitable.

No. BJ15—Boys, 15-inch frame, 20-inch wheels (for ages 5 to 7).................each $35.00

HAND HORN

"Rollfast" **hand horn** is simple and practical. The action is positive, nothing delicate. Weighs 28 ounces; black enamel finish.

No. R. F.—Complete................................each **$1.50**

Bulb Horn—With 8 inch heavily nickeled barrel ....each 1.00

BICYCLE BASKET

Two straps for the handle bar and a metal bracket which is strapped to bicycle head holds this 8 x 14 inch basket rigid and secure. It is made of heavy, galvanized wire woven and twisted over a strong frame.

No. 60—Bike Basket................................each **$1.00**

MISSES' BICYCLES

Misses' Olympic—To give all the advantages possible to the rider, this bicycle has been made with a 17-inch frame and 26-inch wheels. This makes a well-balanced wheel, one easily controlled and propelled. Colors: Red with black head and stripings, mud guards and rims enameled to correspond.

AJ12—Frame 17 inches, wheels 26 inches (for ages from 8 to 10 years)................each $35.00

GIRLS' BICYCLES

Girls' Special—This is a duplicate of the small boys, but in the Misses' Model.

No. BJ16—Girl's, 15-inch frame, 20-inch wheels (for ages 5 to 7)..................each **$35.00**

LADIES' BICYCLES

Lady's Olympic—A well-built bicycle of excellent proportions, and a good coaster. Colors: Blue with black head and stripings, rims and mud guards enameled to correspond.

A70—Frame 20 inches, wheels 28 inches $40.00

1938

No. 41 33—Two-Seater Custer Car—Years ago when we first introduced motor driven automobiles for the use of older children, the children were anxious to try them out but the parents were skeptical. Since then skepticism has diminished and the many cars which have been sold have given satisfaction. We have persisted in developing both electric and gasoline cars with annual improvements. This car embodies all the latest ideas in construction, operation and design. Its Briggs & Stratton single cylinder four cycle $\frac{1}{2}$ horsepower motor is mounted under the ventilated rear deck. It is air cooled and operates direct to rear wheel through a simple planetary transmission having but one speed forward and one reverse controlled by hand lever—no gears. The speed is set to a maximum of 12 miles per hour by set spark and gas controls. It will average at least 50 miles to the gallon. There are but three points of lubrication throughout. The brake operates from the only foot pedal. Overall length 87", width 32", height 32". It is a Two-seater, 4 disc wheels with Goodyear balloon tires. All metal body painted red with black trim....................................**$250.00**

No. 41/65—Streamline Boy's Bicycle (Illustrated)—One of **Columbia's** best. **Columbia** quality is known and needs no further introduction. Fully equipped with electric horn-lite, special reflector, streamlined carrier, kick-up type stand and the feature is the Instrument Panel which has a speedometer and a 24-hour clock in a special housing, only found on **Columbia** Bicycles. The color is a striking carmine and the 3" gothic guards are bright finish. 18" frame with 26" wheels and Balloon Tires........**$49.50**
No. 41/103—(Not illustrated)—As above but equipped for girls in Berkshire Blue. **$48.50**

No. 7/139—"Cadet" Speedometer and Cyclometer—A speedometer and cyclometer made by "Stewart-Warner." Registers speed up to 50 miles per hour and shows total mileage up to 9999 miles. May be used for either 26" or 28" wheels. Attaches to fork of wheel and leaves the handlebar free for other accessories. The feature of the "Cadet" is the "mileage reset"; each trip can be started with 00 mileage...........................**$4.75**

No. 31/55—Bike Watch—A black rubber case which holds and protects the watch is mounted on a metal clasp, which attaches to the handlebar. The white "glownite" numbers on the watch face stand out clearly **$2.25**

No. 40/91—Three Wheel Speedbike—A combination Bicycle and Velocipede, having **chain drive** and three wheels. The advantage of direct drive is immediately in evidence. Maroon frame and red tire rims, other parts nickel plated. Reduced size from saddle to pedal 18". Height to handle bars 28". For Boy or Girl.........................**$18.00**

Interior of Trailer

No. 44/37—Trailer—A completely furnished house on wheels. The interior view reveals folding table, settees that can be made into a bed, stove compartments with doors and table with drawers. Interior walls and furnishings decorated, exterior painted cardinal and maroon. Made of wood and masonite mounted on 5" rubber tired wheels with adjustable draw hook. It measures 30" x 12" x 15". Including special hookup attachment for any velocipede...**$8.75**

No. 40/20—Army Scout Plane—For the budding "young Lindbergh's" first flight along the ground, what could be better practice than this speedy Army Scout Plane. Built of heavy stamped steel finished in maroon baked enamel with ivory, shiny black undergear and gleaming chrome-plated propeller that whizzes around, as the child pedals away. Solid rubber tires make for smooth "flying." Length 46", wing spread 30". For ages 3 to 7 ....**$14.75**

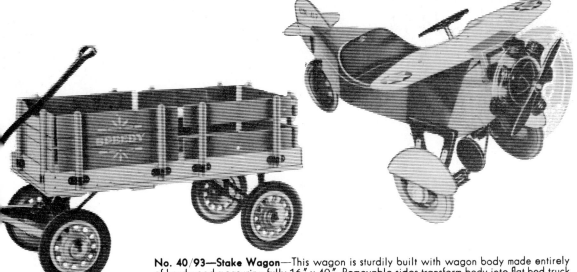

No. 40/93—Stake Wagon—This wagon is sturdily built with wagon body made entirely of hardwood measuring fully 16" x 40". Removable sides transform body into flat bed truck for swift coasting. Strongly supported and stoutly re-enforced with channel steel braces. Roller-bearing steel wheels are of the balloon type. The finish is a luster durable enamel varnish with green and red trim. Plenty of room for two.......................**$8.75**

Sand Carts, with 1 Skin Horse, 50c., $1.00, $1.25, $2.00, $2.75, $3.50, $4.50,
$6.00, $7.

Skin Saddle Horses on platform and rockers combined, $10.00, $14.00, $18.00, $24.

Same, with one forefoot raised 8.0

No. 53 5. **Wooden Push Horse** to steer with reins as shown in cut,
nicely painted, size of horse from floor to saddle 12 in., height
of handle from floor 23 in $4.50

60-66 SKIN COVERED HORSE (Exclusive Import)..................**125.00**
(3 to 6 yrs.)—All children, at one time or another, should own a skin horse
—and here is an imported one with calf-skin cover giving it that crowning
touch. The skin can be brushed and combed and taken care of—a priv-
ilege not enjoyed by the plain wooden horse owners. This handsome steed
rides smoothly, with a back-and-forth motion on rods that swing from a
sturdy and quality made, varnished wooden stand with supports 54" long.
Has real leather saddle. Horse's back 32" from floor. Only selected skins
in their natural colors are used. Express only. Ship. wt. 68 lbs.

27-22 PONY CAR (Exclusive) Ship. wt. 8 lbs..............**10.95**
(1 to 3 yrs.)—An ideal first vehicle for small children. Because of its
low center of gravity, it is safe for little tots and by grasping the
handle bars, his first wobbly steps are steadied. Made entirely of
wood with handsome natural finish and colorful red and blue trim.
21½" x 18" x 12".

60-89 PALOMINO WONDER HORSE (Deluxe) **29.95**
(2 to 5 yrs.)—This handsome charger, moulded of
durable plastic, has the rich coloring of a real Palomino
horse. He is securely suspended in such a way
that a slow easy ride or run of fast action can be enjoyed by the happy rider. Sturdy chrome-finished steel
stirrup makes it easy for even very young range-riders
to "mount up". Chrome-finished tubular steel stand is
36" long. Ship. wt. 20 lbs. Exp. only.

B 60-130 SULKY CYCLE 125.00
(3 to 8 yrs). From the Pampas of
Argentina comes this big, luxurious sulky, with a saucy little
pony, 29" high and covered with
real horsehide. Steering by the
reins, the driver sits in the comfortable bucket seat and pedals.
The easy-operating chain drive
makes sure the pony never gets
tired. Chrome rims, chrome fenders and leather trappings add to
the beautiful appearance of this
exciting plaything. 58" long overall, with removable whip. A child's
dream come true. (Import) EX-
PRESS ONLY. Ship. wt. 57 lbs.

E 60-148 FLASHING HOOK AND LADDER 39.95
(3 to 7½ yrs.) Off to the rescue in this dashing
new Hook and Ladder with two speeds and
flashing red warning light. The easy to shift
Speed-o-matic chain drive helps young fire
fighters make the most of their leg power.
Heavy gauge steel body, finished in red and
white enamel, has rear step for "crew". Other
features are semi-pneumatic tires, simulated
wire wheels with ball bearing construction, 2
wood ladders, clanging bell and of course the
electric blinker light on the hood EXPRESS
ONLY. Ship. wt. 39 lbs.

D 40-4 PUMP SCOOTER (Import) **22.50**
It's fun to go zipping along without even touch-
ing a foot to the ground. That's what a rider on
this new scooter does, just by pumping the
rubber-covered foot pedal. Chain-and-spring
arrangement under platform provides the "go".
Body and tubular steel frame are ruggedly
made with baked enamel finish. Chrome fenders
add a note of luxury. Rolls freely on puncture
proof, semi-pneumatic tires. With brake. 41"
long overall. EXPRESS ONLY. Ship. wt. 20 lbs.

A 860-124 **PEDAL RACER** (Import) Ship. wt. 73 lbs.....**95.00**
(3 to 8 yrs.)—This sleek pedal-driven racer looks speedy even
when it's standing still. Its 51" long streamlined body of pressed
steel is finished in bright red and trimmed with chrome. The
rider sits in a comfortable padded seat and the pedals are adjustable for size. Twin exhausts and racing numbers add to
its professional appearance. Rear-view mirror, horn, and electric lights help make driving it a pleasure. Batteries included
for lights. Express only.

A 819-17 **MERCEDES BENZ RACING CAR** **23.50**
(12 yrs. up)—An exciting 13½" rubber-tired replica in durable
plastic of the famous Grand Prix winner. Gasoline engine powered, completely assembled and ready-to-run, featuring inde-
pendent wheel suspension and adjustable muffler for quiet
operation. Complete with driver, bridle and swivel post for controlled racing, running wire, fuel and battery. Ship. wt. 5 lbs.

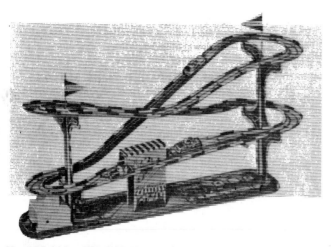

H 811-001 BIG DIPPER ROLLER COASTER (Import) **7.50**
The three 3″ long metal cars climb on each inclined motorized section of the roller coaster track layout. Upon reaching the top they coast speedily down and around twisting turns for long runs. Colorful all metal track layout measures 21″ x 6″ x 11″ and operates on batteries (included). Ship. wt. 4 lbs.

C 818-202 FRICTION-POWERED
MATRA FORD (Import) **8.95**

The newest racer built by SCHUCO. A true-to-scale 10″ long model with fully-sprung individual suspension of front and rear wheels with telescopic absorbers, visibly operating differential, high quality steel chassis with unbreakable plastic body, terrific acceleration. Steering wheel steers front wheels. Friction-type self-winding motor or key winding. Ship. wt. 2 lbs.

A 819-005 BATTERY
RACING SET 15.95

(5 yrs. up)—Easy to set up on carpet or floor, this battery-operated racing set will provide competitive fun for younger children. Figure 8 layout shown measures approximately 5′ in length. Set comes complete with all track including change-over and chicane, hand controls, battery box with batteries and two sleek racing cars. (Import) Ship. wt. 5 lbs.

Hook and Ladder.

ith 2 horses and gong, 21 inches $1.00
" 3 " " " 32 " ....$2.?0
" 3 " " with rubber tire wheels, 30 inches $3.50
" 2 " " gong, 28 in., with aerial ladders extending and moving in any direction..$3.00

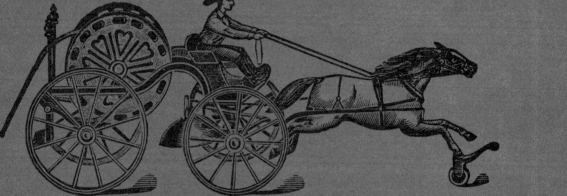

Hose Carriages.

ith 1 horse and bell, 17 inches long...$1.00
" 2 " " " 22 " " " $2.00
" 2 " " rubber tire wheels, 20 inches..$2.50

ansom, with coachman, 14 inches $1.00
" " " " ....25c.
ab, with 1 horse, 14 inches...$1.00

Houses & furnishings

Doll houses and their furnishings have appealed to young and old for centuries. The most famous European examples were fitted with such exquisitely detailed objects that one wonders how often children were allowed to play with them. The Schwarz examples of the 1920s and 1930s were sturdier and designed for play. The architecture is clearly suburban, quaint and eclectic. The large house of 1923 and the smaller of 1932 suggest that middle-class homes were in a process of becoming less imposing and more informal in that period. Furniture was more often made in traditional designs than the modern. Kitchens were stocked with devices that appealed to little girls. There was equipment for cooking, scrubbing and acting out the housewife's role. Toy sinks have water tanks to provide running water for the young dishwasher.

For the future homemaker with high hopes, a toy swimming pool equipped with slides and showers was available as a Schwarz exclusive of 1936 when private pools were rare. The girl or boy content with more modest surroundings was offered gardening sets that often included materials for real gardening.

The 1957 catalogue included a set that had the fittings of a grocery shop that was stocked with an impressive assortment of real edibles which many children were able to use to create unbelievable messes. After all the boxes were opened, there was a cash register that could be used to add up the damages. The toy-sized working soda fountain inspired more careful activity because it was used to produce authentic sodas and sundaes.

Play furnishings come in three sizes. Doll houses are generally small and require special dolls and trappings. Ordinary dolls are sometimes supplied with chairs and tables that would be an intermediate scale, while children's play furniture is still larger. All three scales afford the same delight to those who enjoy using the furnishings to achieve a sense of reality in their play.

Stables, some with wooden and some with skin horses, 65c., $1.25, $
$2.25, $3.00, $4.00, $4.50, $5.50, $6.50, $10.00, $12.00, $13.50,

Above, 34 inches high.   Price, $7.50

Warehouses....... 2.25, $3.50, $4.75, $5.50, $6.00, $16.00

No. 5603F—2-Story House with 3 plainly furnished rooms, 1 room in attic, porch, veranda and windows, decorated with flowers. 25 inches long, 25 inches high, 12 inches deep $18.00

No. 5600F—2-Story House with 3 plainly furnished rooms and hall, also 2 rooms in attic, large veranda decorated with flowers. 18 inches long, 21 inches high, 11 inches deep 13.50

No. 5601F—Same, but larger. 22 x 27 x 12 inches 20.00

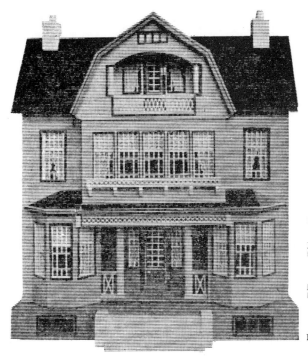

No. 5609

No. 5609—3-story House, 5 rooms, unfurnished, stairway with hall. Measurements 31 x 15 x 30 inches $35.00
Furnished in every detail 65.00

No. 5610—4-story House. 8 rooms, unfurnished. stairway with large hall on every floor. Measurements 46 x 20 x 34 inches 75.00
Furnished in every detail 150.00

No. 5193—Very large Doll House with porch and veranda, big stairway with 2 large halls on one side, 4 large rooms on the other side, 38 inches wide, 41 inches high. 20 inches deep, unfurnished 65.00
Furnished in every detail 125.00

GREEN HOUSES

A miniature green house is good for plants and children. The glass and wooden framed structure with hinged roof fosters the growth of young plants. Instructions on the care of plants is included.

No. 175—16¾ x 10¾ x 10½ inches ....$ 3.00
No. 176—25½ x 15½ x 15 inches 7.50
No. 177—36½ x 22½ x 20 inches 15.00

GARDEN CART

Body made of sheet metal painted in green, has water tank. The cart is trimmed with a great number of garden tools, a basket, sprinkler and pail. Made in two sizes:

No. 2140/0—Size of body 14½ x 9 inches $13.50
No. 2140/1—Size of body 18½ x 12 inches 20.00

LITTLE GARDENER

No. 181—Containing 12 miniature clay flower pots, 12 pans and 12 different packages of seed, sprinkling can, shovel, rake, hoe, pail, can of fertilizer and sieve.................$2.50

No. 180—Containing six miniature flower pots with gay pans to rest in, watering pail and spade and half dozen selected packages of seeds. $1.00

MINIATURE GARDENING SERIE

This latest educational toy enables the amateur gardener to plan his garden in a thoroughly practical manner, laying the beds, paths, arches, etc., and filling them with a large variety of plants (each one is an individual flower) in full bloom, arranging and rearranging his designs at will. Sets made entirely of lead, realistically painted.

No. 13 MG $3.00
No. 12 MG 2.00

ENGLISH TYPE COTTAGE

No. AA-3—A cottage built for two—though the three rooms are so large, more could be accommodated. It is lighted with electricity and has real glass windows. House is built of wood with imitation stucco finish in buff with green trim and a deeply sloping roof, stained dark red. The kitchen has colored tile linoleum on the floor—the other floors are "hardwood". The back is open. Cottage measures 34" long, 18" wide and 19" high. Electric cord and plug included for house current. As illustrated $17.50

LIBRARY

For the library in the most favored style of American furniture. All of mahogany.
No. B-300—Book Case, $1.50; No. B-501—Card Table, $1.00; No. B-145—Desk, $3.50; No. B-227—Windsor Hoop Chair, $2.00; No. B-225—Windsor Chair, $1.50; No. B-1607—Desk Set, $0.65; No. B-1100—Banjo Clock, $1.00; No. B-1675—Screen, $1.00; No. B-146—Highboy, $3.00; Rug, $0.65.

VICTORIAN BED ROOM

Mahogany furniture of the quaint Victorian style.
No. B-105—Spool Bed, $2.50; No. B-144—Bureau, $2.75; No. B-229—Chair, $1.00; No. B-514—Spool Stand, $1.35; No. B-1806—Silhouette Picture, $0.45; No. B-1102—Terry Clock, $0.65; Braided Rag Rug, $1.10.

CHIPPENDALE DINING ROOM

Complete for the correct dining room in beautiful Chippendale style. All mahogany.
No. B-301—Corner Cupboard, $2.25; No. B-431—Sideboard, $2.50; No. B-503—Drop Leaf Table, $1.50; No. B-210—Chair, $0.90; No. B-211—Arm Chair, $1.25; No. B-508—Side Table, $0.75; No. B-1100—Banjo Clock, $1.00; No. B-1101—Grandfather Clock, $1.25; Rug, $0.65.

KITCHEN

Cheerful and gay as kitchen furniture should be, painted in pretty green shade.
No. B-5—Kitchen Cabinet, $1.50; No. B-8501/6—Side Table, $0.40; No. B-8501/4—Kitchen Table, $0.50; No. B-8501/5—Kitchen Chair, $0.35; No. B-8350—Sink, $1.00; No. B-832—Iron Ice Box, white, $0.75; No. B-870—Iron Range, white, $0.50.

ELECTRIC RANGE

No. C-206—Durably constructed, finished in green baked enamel, ivory trim, back panel has attractive silhouette design. Furnished with 6 aluminum utensils. An added feature is the heat indicator. Size 12½" x 9" x 6½". Ready for house current..**$1.75**

No. C-24—(Illustrated.) A large size range, ruggedly constructed. Finished in green baked enamel, with ivory trim, and polished nickel. Silhouette design on back. Furnished with aluminum tea kettle, cake pan and pie plate. Size 14" x 12" x 6". Ready for house current..**$4.50**

KITCHEN SINK

No. AA-9023—Dishwashing becomes a pleasure with this toy kitchen sink—for doll's dishes or playtime teathings. Nicely constructed of wood, painted cream with green "tile" facing. Imitation granite drain boards and a real copper sink with drain and real faucet, supplied with water from tank at back. Sink is 22" high from the floor and the shelves reach to height of 45". When hinged shelf at side is open, overall width is 40". The two long shelves and four smaller ones hold a complete array of kitchenware. Aluminum steamer, saucepan, 2 kettles, tea kettle, coffee percolator, strainer, tea set for 6 and knives, forks and spoons. There are all kinds of brushes for bottles and pans, an aluminum dishpan, wire dish strainer, dish cloth, dish towel, rubber apron and cookie cutters, wooden rolling pin and bread board, and a real 164 page cook book. **Designed and sold exclusively by us.** Complete.....................................**$32.00**

DISH WASHING OUTFIT

No. C-8410—For the more serious moments of miniature housekeeping is this practical kitchen outfit which includes rubber apron, washcloth, dish towel, soap and 5 dishwashing utensils...**$2.00**

Iron Stoves, to burn coal, very complete, $1.00, $2.00, $2.25, $3.00, $5.00, $6.50

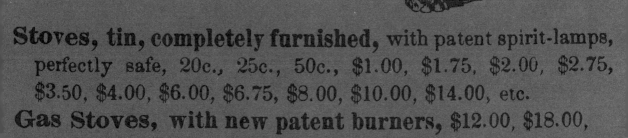

Stoves, tin, completely furnished, with patent spirit-lamps, perfectly safe, 20c., 25c., 50c., $1.00, $1.75, $2.00, $2.75, $3.50, $4.00, $6.00, $6.75, $8.00, $10.00, $14.00, etc.

Gas Stoves, with new patent burners, $12.00, $18.00,

1936

The Four Rooms—This arrangement has its advantages for the light housekeeper, there being but a kitchen, bath room, bed room and combination dining and living room. The wood outside is painted white with slanting green roof. The inside is fitted with a full set of doors, is electrically lighted for 110 volt circuit and is fully wall papered and floor covered. DESIGNED BY SCHWARZ.

No. 42/37—Unfurnished **$12.00**

No. 42/44—The same 4 rooms each furnished as if by an interior decorator with complete set of furniture, curtains and draperies also set of doll house dolls, of parents, children and maid. **$32.00**

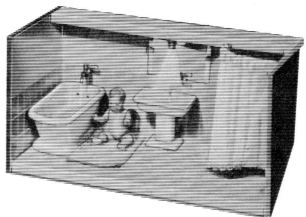

No. 24/55—Bathroom—Modern young housekeepers will like this attractive bathroom of colored metal, faced with white and blue tile. You just fill the flat water tank at the back, and then, with a turn of the real faucet on bathtub or basin you actually have running water. But the electric light is the real feature. It lights the mirror beautifully for Dolly to do her "primping." Complete with wash cloth, towel and soap. Room 12½ inches by 6½ inches by 6½ inches. Bisque doll included. MADE EXCLUSIVELY FOR SCHWARZ **$4.50**

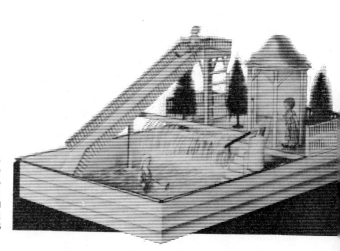

No. 24/52—Swimming Pool—For the doll's playtime hours what could be jollier than this swimming pool with its thrilling long slide? The tank may be filled with water and then the shower actually works. Includes 3 bisque dolls and towels. Size of tank 12 inches by 18 inches, made of fine metal done in pretty pastel coloring. DESIGNED BY AND MANUFACTURED FOR SCHWARZ EXCLUSIVELY SCHWARZ **$8.75**

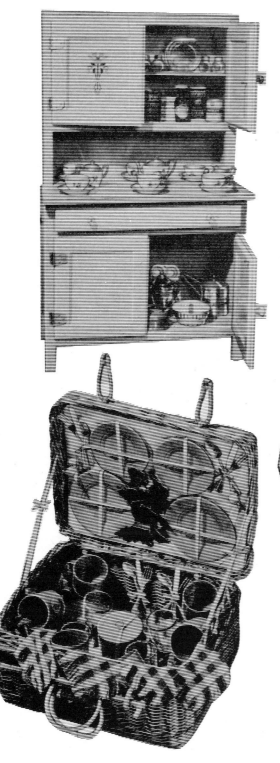

No. 44/73—Kitchen Cabinet—This kitchen cabinet is just what little housekeepers have been waiting for. It is strongly put together of plywood finished in ivory and green with colorful painted floral decoration and has generous sized working shelf of the natural wood, just like the big one in Mother's kitchen. At the top there's the double-shelved compartment with an ample supply of groceries, well known brands of cocoa, preserves, vegetables, soups, etc., also a cookie jar and two sets of salt and pepper shakers. And in the bottom compartment there's a double-boiler, tea kettle, percolator, muffin pan and a cake form. An extra drawer, too. A complete china tea service for six: cups, saucers and plates. Cabinet size over all 23 x 13 x 41 inches. SCHWARZ' OWN EXCLUSIVE COMBINATION.
$24.00

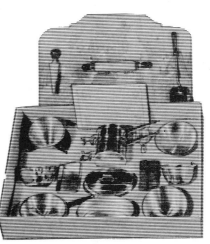

No. 24/4—Cooking Set—For the very serious moments of cooking, little housekeepers will need this practical set. There's the rolling pin and board for first steps in baking, two baking pans and some cookie molds, a potato masher, a saucepan, a scoop, a frying pan, a food press, double boiler and roasting pan. In decorative box 20 x 14 inches. Set made of aluminum. . . . **$2.00**
No. 24/12/3—Hamper with Complete Luncheon Service—A real delight to the exacting "little hostess," this lovely natural willow hamper just full of dainty things to set the prettiest and most appetizing luncheon table. Includes the famous "Alice in Wonderland" tea set (see No. 24/9 on this page) in bright red to match the red-and-white fringed gingham cloth, 24 x 30 inches, and the 4 napkins, also 4 water glasses with blue foot and rim and 4 knives, forks and spoons. Hamper 12 x 9½ x 7 inches with carrying handle. EXCLUSIVE WITH SCHWARZ. **$7.50**

B 60-32 KITCHEN STOVE **49.50**
25½" x 15½" x 28½" high. Oven doors open
and close. Has two bottom drawers for
storing the eight pieces of cooking equipment and there is a simulated timer. Hidden red bulbs make two front burners glow
realistically red when handles are turned
"on". Batteries included. Wt. 39 lbs. Exp.

C 60-42 LARGE KITCHEN SINK **72.50**
34½" x 18" x 42" high overall, with storage
space in its many drawers, a picture window with curtains and shelves. Water
supplied by gravity from a concealed tank.
Equipped with a cake box set and salad
set plus dish washing set. 75 lbs. Exp.

D 60-28 KITCHEN REFRIGERATOR 50.00
Two separate doors, one for the freezer and
one for the main refrigerator, with each
compartment having an interior automatic
light (battery operated). 20" x 15" x 40"
high, with three handy door shelves and
two removable deep shelves, and 21 us-
able items. Batteries included. 41 lbs. Exp.

J 12-48 MIXI-BAKE DRINK SET **4.95**
(4 yrs. up)—Just push the button in the red
plastic base of this battery-driven electric
mixer and the agitator will whip up a
frothy milk shake or batter for a tempting
batch of cookies, 16 oz. tumbler, mixing
bowl, biscuit pan, measuring cup, straws,
2 tumblers, mixing spoon, 2 cake pans.
Ship. wt. 3 lbs. Batteries Included.

F 12-38 ELEC. WASH MACHINE 6.00
(5 yrs. up) A toy washing machine is a time-tested favorite that retains its appeal over a long period. This is a scaled-down model of Moms' agitator-type, operating on 2 flashlight batteries. Simple off-on switch operates the 12" high machine mounted on ball-bearing casters. Adjustable wringer, made of steel and hard rubber rollers offers extra play value. BATTERIES NOT INCLUDED. See below. Ship wt. 4 lbs.
2-1 SET OF 2 BATTERIES FOR ABOVE .40

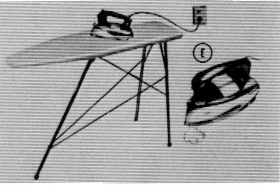

E 27-158 STEAM IRON AND BOARD 6.95
(5 yrs. up) Ironing Day is fun to the proud young "mother" who does dollys' wash with this new set, featuring a steam iron that actually produces steam. And just like Mommys', it has an automatic steam cut-off, if it is not held in the ironing position. The all-steel perforated ironing board opens and closes in one simple operation. Tubular legs have rubber tips. 27" long and 22" high. Cotton cover has drawstring to assure snug fit. UL approved. Ship. wt. 6 lbs.

D 11-38 SUSIE ROBETTE Wt. 4 lbs. **7.95**
(3 years up) The first female robot is, as might be expected, a fastidious housekeeper. She sweeps, dusts and vacuums, as she moves forward, circles to the right or left. 11" tall and made of tough high-impact plastic with metallic finish, Susie is feminine enough to wear a pony tail of coppered wire. She operates on 2 flashlight batteries and her bow encloses the "off-on" switch. Her hands are equipped with plastic grips to clutch whatever accessory she is using. BATTERIES NOT INCLUDED. See below.
2-1 SET OF BATTERIES FOR ABOVE .40

A 20-56 HOUSECLEANING SET 5.00
(3 to 10 yrs.)—Mother is sure to find her own work lighter when her little helper has her very own set of cleaning equipment to lend a willing hand. This set of 16 pieces includes both cleaning and dishwashing equipment, featuring such "necessities" as dishpan, drain tray, apron, carpet cleaner, dry mop, sponge mop with wringer and hand duster. Ship. wt. 5 lbs.

1957

H 60-12 LARGE GROCERY STORE 42.50
(4 to 10 yrs.)—For imaginative play, running a busy grocery store is really wonderful fun! There's a scale, cash register, a telephone to take orders to be filled from the "inventory" of well-known brands of foods. Large back shelves 36" high, 29" wide and 27" deep overall with 18 drawers for staples. Wt. 40 lbs. Express only. (Exclusive.)

J 4-77 CASH REGISTER **3.95**
It's fun to "play store". This two-drawer register has a Tally Recorder for doing the "figuring" — it erases itself, never needs paper. Push lever opens cash drawer, automatically ringing bell. Steel construction with chrome front. Metal play money included. Ship. wt. 5 lbs.

E 11-8 COCA-COLA DISPENSER **3.50**
(5 yrs. up)—Here's a real treat for youngsters, a home edition of a Coke fountain that looks very professional and it really works. Just insert the bottle, tip the lever, then out pours the drink into one of 2 clear plastic glasses. Machine will hold any standard 6 oz. sized bottle. Made of bright red plastic 6 x 9 x 10". Ship. wt. 4 lbs.

E 60-3 ICE CREAM FOUNTAIN **39.75**
(Exclusive) A trip to an ice cream fountain has always been a big treat for youngsters but few of them have had the thrill of working behind the counter, serving sodas, sundaes, frappes and all manner of delicious concoctions. With this unusual toy everything but the ice cream is provided —banana split and sundae dishes, spoons, glasses, holders, and scoop, all in durable colored plastic, plus flavoring, chocolate syrup, grape juice, paper napkins, doilies, straws and a battery-operated mixer. The well made wood fountain, finished in red and white with chrome trim, has a roomy 36" long counter, and 3 spinning stools. Built-in shelf accommodates all the equipment. 41" deep overall. Batteries included Ship. wt. 52 lbs. EXPRESS ONLY.

cut $7.50

Others :   5.00   6.75   10.00   12.00
    14.00   15.00   18.00   28.00   48.00

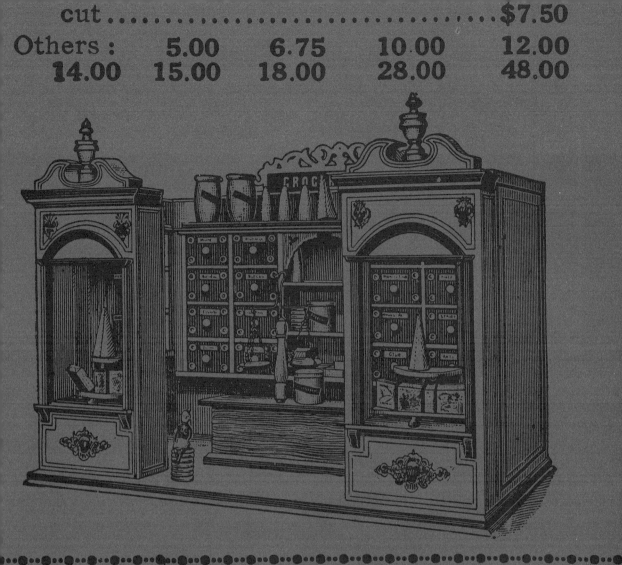

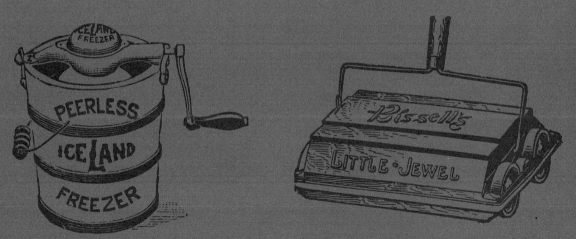

MODEL
ICE CREAM FREEZER

Sufficient to make 1 pint of
cream $1.25
Ice Chipper . . . . 25c.

CHILDREN'S
CARPET SWEEPERS

25c., 50c., 75c., $1.25, $2.50

Ships & airplanes & trains

Traveling has always been a source of fascination for children. Fifty years ago, riding or sailing, on the ground, on the sea, or in the air were adventures more often heard about than experienced first hand. Today, distances are less important and families are more mobile as the quest for jobs inspires relocating.

In 1912 the large passenger liners were for trips that affluent parents made more often alone than with their offspring, but everyone spoke of the wonder world of the great luxury liners. The children of poor immigrants heard of the trials of traveling aboard these ships on the lower decks which were for those who could afford only the lowest rates. Before 1914 threats of war stimulated arms races that affected the toy market as readily as the real world. Christmas, 1912, found many boys playing with torpedo boats, submarines and the like. Those who preferred to encourage more peaceful interests in their children could buy models of pleasurecraft. Motor boats, then unlike now, were rare, since most families with summer homes on the water owned row boats or canoes.

Miniature railroads were made with such refinement that it is difficult to decide whether they were toys or scale models to be admired rather than used for play. An impressive array of the better-known locomotives and the freight and passenger cars they pulled were available to aspiring engineers. Kits with parts to make airplanes that could fly were popular toys of the 1930s. The lighter models had rubber band motors while the heavier ones were equipped with gas engines.

Most toys follow the latest trends but you find old-fashioned boats, trains and planes pictured in catalogues as early as the 1950s. Nostalgia is a factor stimulated by television that has revived the popularity of the old-style steamboats and Word War I fighter planes.

Fine Model Yachts		30-inch	36-inch	43-inc
The Defender Model	....	$16.50	$28.00	$33.00

Sailboats, cheaper grades.........25c., 50c., 65c., 85c., $1.0

Rowboats to attach to sailboats, ..6c., 10c., 12c., 15c., 25c

Fine Model Yachts with Fin Keel. (See Cut.)

12-inch	15-inch	18-inch	21-inch	24-inch	30-inch	36-inc
$3.00	$4.50	$6.75	$8.00	$10.00	$12.00	$15.75

Plainer		12-inch	15-inch	18-inch	24-inc
		$1.75	$2.50	$3.50	$5.00

FINE PASSENGER BOATS

Beautifully finished. Excellent models. 24 inches................$10.00
    Like cut, 26 inches.........$12.00   28 inches...................15.00
Plainer, 8 inches............... .50   10 inches................... 1.00
    13 inches ...... $2.00 16 inches.......$4.00 18 inches 5.50

MECHANICAL PIKE

When wound up and placed in water, the fish dives and rises alternately. Floats when run down.

14 inches...............$1.50

FINE WAR-SHIPS

Made of tin and highly painted and lacquered, like cut, 22 inches long...$7.50

Similar styles:

   10½ inches...........$1.00   17 inches........................ 3.00
   13 inches................... 2.00   19 inches....... .... 5.00

TORPEDO BOATS

Very good reproduction of the latest U. S. N. type.

No.
221.—Length 11 in. .... $ 2.00
222.—Length 13 in. 2.50
223.—Length 17 in. 4.25
231.—Length 21 in. 6.75

232.—Length 23 in. $10.00
233.—Length 28 in. 15.00
234.—Length 39 in. 25.00

SUBMARINES

The two larger types dive and rise automatically.

No.
100.—Length 10 in. .... $ 1.25
190.—Length 11 in. 2.25

191.—Length 13 in. $5.75
192.—Length 18 in. 10.00

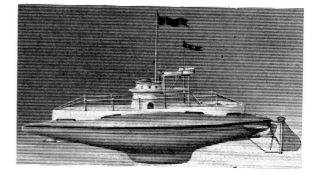

CRUISERS

No.
441.—Length 18 in. .... $ 7.00
442.—Length 22 in. 12.00

No.
444.—Length 29 in. $18.00
446.—Length 36 in. 38.00

MOTOR BOATS

Type of the Racing Motor Boat.

No.
31.—Length 11 in. ...$2.25
32.—Length 15 in. ... 3.75
33.—Length 20 in. ..; 5.00
34.—Length 24 in. ... 6.00

BOATS, to run by Steam

Red hull, brass border.

Launches, like cut, 12 inches long......**$2.25**   Launches, like cut, 16 inches long......**3.75**
Launches, like cut, 20 inches long.................................**$6.00**

SELF-FIRING GUNBOATS

The mechanism is so arranged that the boat will go out a little ways, fire a shot and return to the starting point.

No.
381.—Length 12 in. .....**$ 4.50**
382.—Length 16 in. 6.50

383.—Length 19 in. **$10.00**
(Fires two shots)

FERRY BOATS

No.
1.—Length 14 in. **$3.00**
2.—Length 16 in. 4.75
3.—Length 20 in. 9.50

1931

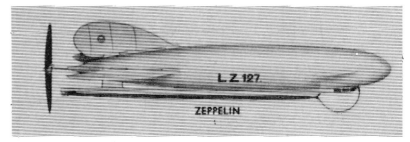

L Z 127

ZEPPELIN

ZEPPELIN (It Flies)

This is the first lighter-than-air flying model. It will surprise you by staying in the air from about 300 to 500 feet. The balloon is made of a specially prepared airtight fabric in a realistic dull grey finish. The rubberband motor is good for many, many trips. Flying instructions are included, very simple to handle. Length overall 38 inches................$13.50

SWIMMING DOLL

No. 601—One-piece suit, in assorted colors. When wound up it swims with Australian crawl, 8 in. long $1.50

DIVER

No. 545-E—Down went McGinty . . . but he always comes up—our McGinty. All he asks you to do is to pump air through the rubber tube and he'll dive and rise until you get dizzy from watching him. 7 in. tall and he is holding an electric hand lantern (battery included) $3.00

No. 545—If you can do without the electric hand lantern you can get him for 1.75

545E

WHALE

No. 111—Whales are not usually good companions but this has proven his popularity being 15 inches long with a flopping tail and a real water spout; spring motor driven $12.00

545

mechanical parts of high power, and the tracks, a large variety of which are furnished with every train, are of proved shape, preventing derailments if properly joined. Extra track can be added from time to time. We can justly that any of these trains, with the extra accessories as shown by the illustrations on this page, as Stations, Depots, Tunnels, etc. will prove a highly interesting and instructive toy for boys of any age.

—— **Complete Catalogue sent on application.** ——

Mechanical Railroad Trains $3.50, $6.00, $8.00, $10.00, $14.00, $20.00, $32.00

lighter material $1.00, $2.00, $4.00, $7.50

Locomotive.   Passenger Car.   Cattle Car.

Railroad Crossing.   Freight Depot, $3.75.

Guardhouse, $3.50.   Arc Light.   Tunnel.

MECHANICAL TRAINS OF LIGHTER MATERIAL.

			No. AR
			" AVE
No. 36/6/1.	Loco., tender, one car, circular track, 20½ in.	$1.00	" AE
" 604/1.	Loco., with brake, tender, 2 cars, oval track, 3 ft. 5 in. x 30 in.	3.00	" AR
" 1090/4a.	Loco, tender, 2 cars, oval track, 4 ft. 4 in.		" AVE

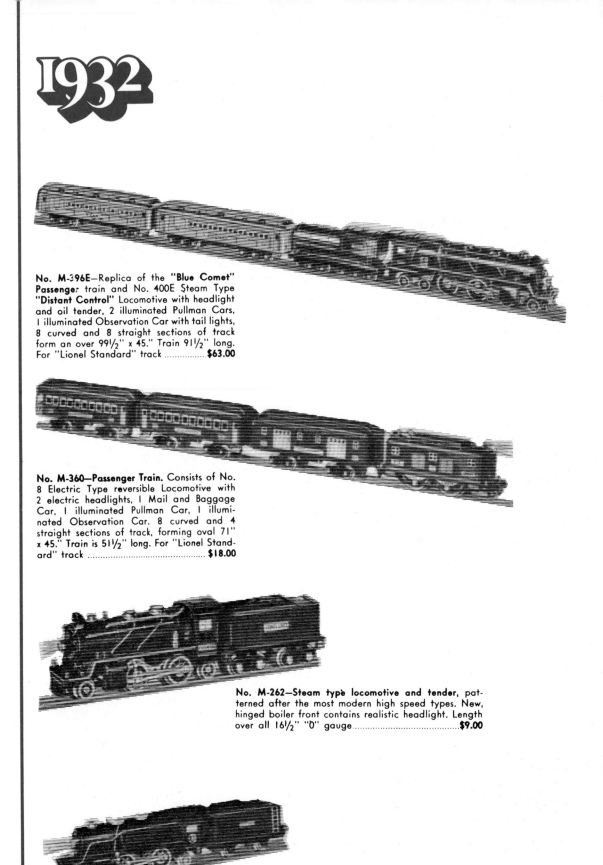

No. M-396E—Replica of the "Blue Comet" Passenger train and No. 400E Steam Type "Distant Control" Locomotive with headlight and oil tender, 2 illuminated Pullman Cars, 1 illuminated Observation Car with tail lights, 8 curved and 8 straight sections of track form an over 99½" x 45." Train 91½" long. For "Lionel Standard" track **$63.00**

No. M-360—Passenger Train. Consists of No. 8 Electric Type reversible Locomotive with 2 electric headlights, 1 Mail and Baggage Car, 1 illuminated Pullman Car, 1 illuminated Observation Car. 8 curved and 4 straight sections of track, forming oval 71" x 45." Train is 51½" long. For "Lionel Standard" track **$18.00**

No. M-262—Steam type locomotive and tender, patterned after the most modern high speed types. New, hinged boiler front contains realistic headlight. Length over all 16½" "0" gauge..**$9.00**

No. M-259—New Steam type Reversible "0" gauge Locomotive and tender, excelling in workmanship and detail. Concealed headlight, colored pilot lights and illuminated number plate. Overall length 15½"....**$6.75**

No. M-409E—Passenger Train, consists of No. 381E powerful, electric type, reversible by **"distant control"** Locomotive, with electric headlights, 2 illuminated Pullman cars with luxurious inner details, 1 illuminated Observation Car, 8 curved and 10 straight sections of track forms oval 114" x 45". Train is 86½" long. For "Lionel Standard" Track **$58.50**

No. M-386E—Freight Train. Consists of No. 384E Steam Type **Distant Control** Locomotive with electric headlight, with tender, 1 Gondola Car with barrels, 1 Cattle Car, 1 illuminated Caboose, 8 curved and 4 straight sections of track, forming oval 71" x 45". Train is 60½" long. For "Lionel Standard" track. **$28.35**

No. M-392E—New Steam Type "Distant Control" Locomotive and **Tender.** Latest model with double pilot trucks, heavy trailer trucks and double action piston rods. Powerful concealed headlight, red and green pilot lights and glowing fire box. Overall length 25". For "Lionel Standard" Track.........................**$31.50**

No. M-400E—"Distant Control" Steam Type Locomotive and oil **Tender.** This most powerful of all model steam type locomotives will pull an incredibly long train of cars. It has the hinged boiler front with automatic lock which conceals and protects lamp. Colorful pilot lights and glowing firebox add realism. Overall length 30½". For "Lionel Standard" track **$40.50**

No. 10/134—Ryan Construction Set—Our Ryan Construction Set model reproduces in every detail an actual flying ship as built by the Ryan Aeronautical Company of San Diego. Colored a brilliant silver and featuring the exclusive Keel fusilage construction, this kit has an abundance of every material necessary to construct a perfect model. Size: span 23 inches, length 17 inches. Lightness of material insures long flights, rubber band motor. **$2.50**

No. 10/133—Waco Construction Set—Same general specifications as in Ryan Set above except color is orange and cream with black details and this has 22½ inch span with 16½ inch length. **$2.75**

No. 10/155—Ships Aloft—A Construction Book for Future Flyers, By Clayton Knight and Harold Platt. A book for everybody who is interested in aviation—and who is not? Like its popular predecessor, SHIP AHOY!, it is a construction book, consisting of extremely dramatic and colorful lithographs of the Pan American China Clipper, the Douglas Airliner, the new Boeing Army Bomber, and a formation of Navy pursuit ships, each against its appropriate background—ocean, tropical island, battle fleet, or mountain range. For each illustration there is a set of parts, with instructions for cutting out and pasting on the picture to give a relief effect both stunning and realistic. The pictures are reproduced in five colors, from original paintings by Clayton Knight, who is famous for his drawings of aviation subjects. The spiral binding allows the pictures to be removed for framing. Ages ten and up. Boards (12¾ x 18¾). **$2.50**

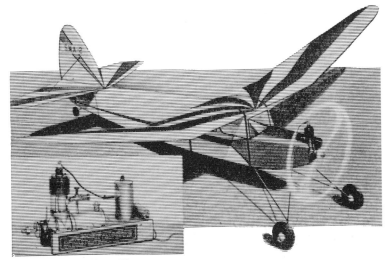

No. 10/154—"Red Zephyr" Gas Model Construction Kit —The kit is complete in every respect, and includes many finished parts that greatly simplify construction. When powered with the below described Gasoline Motor this beautiful ship takes off the ground within 25 feet and climbs steadily to a height of several hundred feet coming down again to a graceful 3 point landing. Wingspan of this big ship 72 inches. (less motor). **$5.95**

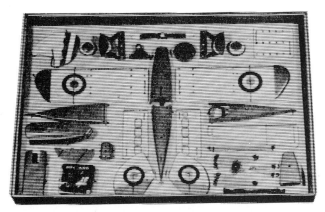

"Meccano" Airplane Building Sets—Good news! The famous "Meccano" now branches forth into airplane building sets. Instructive, interesting and the finished products are so tremendously worthwhile. Just imagine assembling planes complicated as the ships pictured at right, but they're just two which can be built with these sets. All pieces of metal brilliantly enameled in assorted colors, all parts complete, nuts, bolts, screws, rods, etc., even to the rubber-tired wheels and a pilot. Order by number for the three sets featured:

No. 11/77—Builds models with 17 inch wing spread, also includes instructions to construct 6 different planes such as a training biplane, a low wing monoplane, a high wing monoplane, a standard light plane, a single-seater and many more. In box 17 x 11 inches. **$4.00**

No. 11/38—Builds models with 18½ inch wing spread and includes special instructions for constructing about 44 types of planes and educational data on such subjects as: How an Airplane Flies, Explanations of motors, parts, etc., and even a Short History of planes. In box 21 x 15 inches. **$7.50**

No. 11/40—Our Best Set with many more pieces to build many more planes. In box 23 x 20 inches. **$12.00**

No. 9 – 31—U-Control Assembly Set (Fireball) (Class B)—A plane that you can fly in your back-yard due to unique "U-Control". Flight of plane is controlled right from your hand with the U-Control which is a U-shaped long wire attached to plane. Easy to assemble as all parts are shaped and of balsa wood. Requires less than half the time ordinary models take to build. Wingspan 35". Motor not included. See below for motor. **$7.95**

No. 31 – 417—Ohlsson "23" Motor—A powerful rugged little motor with enclosed ignition timer and visible fuel supply. Most suitable for above model. **$18.00**

U-Control Assembly Set
(Fireball)

Ohlsson "23" Motor

No. 9 – 60—Parachute Plane Construction Set—With automatic trapdoor release. Contains all necessary material, including machine-cut propeller, ball-bearing washer, tissue, formed wire parts, all parts required for constructing parachute and automatic trapdoor release, ready-made pilot, and full size easily understood plan. Construction is simple; anyone with little experience can build this 40" wingspan Parachute Plane. The trapdoor automatically opens after plane is about 40 seconds in the air, and parachute with pilot slowly drifts earthward. Rubber band motor included.

$1.50

Class A "Schwarz Special" Construction Sets—Here are two kits extraordinary! The most complete of their kind—each including that wonderful little "Atom" Gas Motor that will take the plane (when finished) on many a worthwhile flight. Parts have been carefully selected to combine strength and speed in flight, and to withstand frequent usage and most landing accidents. The pneumatic wheels are noteworthy—and there's an extra supply of paper covering material, also necessary wood, dope, glue, flight timer, brush and knife. Full size plan.

No. 10 – 81—Cabin Model, wingspan 37". Complete with motor. **$18.50**

No. 10 – 82—Contest Model, wingspan 33". Complete with motor. 18.50

SCHWARZ
SPECIALS

No. 10 – 82   Contest Model   No. 10 – 81   Cabin Model

echanical Rail Road Trains,

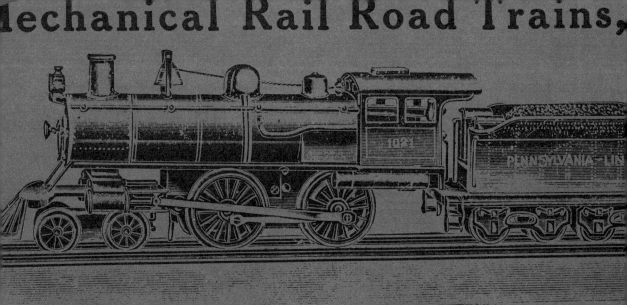

LOCO, No. A E 1021

Fine quality, 4 axles, reversible, with brake, for track No. 1.

O, No. A E 1020. Smaller, for track O.

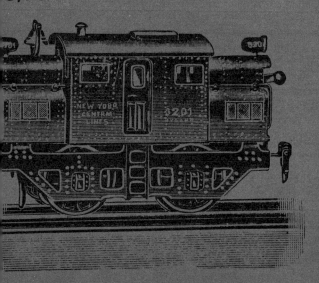

LOCO, A V R

hape of Electric Locomotive, reversible,
with brake, 2 axles.
D has 3 axles.

Finest Workmanship, at prices
Locomotives are of high power a
ed in a manner making derailmen
A variety of track furnished with
new equipment from time to ti
Rail Road System may be built
keep everything imaginable in R

EXTRA CARS OF EVERY DESCRIP
TRACKS, SWITCHES, STATI
BRIDGES, TUNNELS, I

Separate Price-List Mailed

(For Description of Locomotives see cuts above

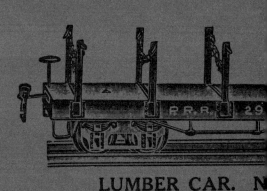

LUMBER CAR. N

210/2.   Loco., with brake, tenc
7 in. x 2 ft. 5 in. (gaug
Loco, with brake, te

E 18-333 "NATCHEZ" MISSISSIPPI RIVER BOAT KIT Ship. wt. 6 lbs...... **9.95**
A stately 22" model of one of the fastest and most famous Mississippi River
packets. In this 365 part all-plastic kit all the beauty and detail of the original
are accurately reproduced in exact scale. Complete with stand, less cement

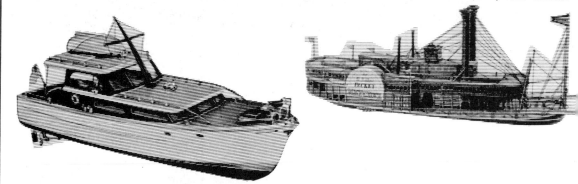

H 18-334 MOTORIZED "WHEELER" SPORT CRUISER KIT Ship. wt. 4 lbs..... **11.95**
An accurate 21" scale model of the luxurious sport cruiser made by the Wheeler
Boat Company, reproduced in plastic kit form, 1/2" to the foot. Includes two electric motors for operation in water and comes complete with display stand and
cement, less batteries. (see below).
2-19 SET OF FOUR BATTERIES.. **.80**

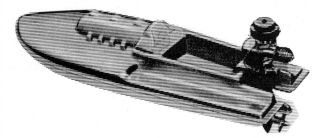

J 18-239 CORVETTE HYDRO SPEEDBOAT Ship. wt 4 lbs................. **16.95**
(12 yrs. up)—The thrill of speedboating is brought right to the youngsters by
this newly designed 18" plastic fully assembled single-step hydroplane, powered
by a gasoline fuelled automatic-starting outboard motor. Capable of speeds to
20 knots on a rudder controlled course. Complete, less fuel and battery. (see "H"
page 57).

K 18-318 S. S. UNITED STATES ASSEMBLY KIT Ship. wt. 8 lbs.......... **10.00**
A detailed plastic assembly kit of over 200 parts, right down to davits and masts,
complete with stand and specification plaque. 29" long and 7" high, she comes
with twin lights to light up on house current. Cement and lighting cord included.

D 18-223 NAVAL LANDING FORCE KIT Wt. 3 lbs.....**5.95**
(9 yrs. up)—The capture of fortified enemy-held island out-
posts was greatly facilitated during World War II through
the use of this formidable landing force unit. All-plastic
kit includes the speedy "P.T." Torpedo Boat, the dogged
L.S.T. Landing Craft, and the powerful supporting Aircraft
Carrier "Wasp", ranging in length from 15" to 20". Complete,
less cement.

E 18-111 WORLD WAR I FIGHTER KIT Ship. wt. 3 lbs. **4.75**
(9 yrs. up)—Six 1/4" plastic scale model kits depicting some
of the most familiar World War I airplanes. Included are the
Fokker Triplane, the Fokker D-7, the Albatross D-3, the SE-5
Scout, the Sopwith Camel, and the Nieuport II. Wingspan
6 1/2" to 7 1/2". Figures and cement included.

F 19-110 JET GUARDIANS OF THE AIR KIT Wt. 3 lbs. **4.95**
(9 yrs. up)—American air power is symbolized in this jet
plane set, including the long-range Northrup Interceptor, the
Convair Delta Wing Interceptor, the Super Saber, the Martin
B-57 Bomber and the Voodoo F-101 fighter. All plastic, wing-
spans 6" to 9 3/8". Cement swivel bases included.

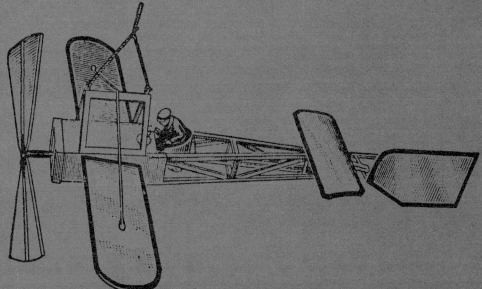

No. 6110 B. MONOPLANE

Aluminum frame with Silk wings, 31 in. long................$3.50

No. 5956 Leblanc. Similar to 6110 B Monoplane. Double Aluminum frame with Silk wings, 32 in. long............ 3.50

No. 6112. Same as 6110 B, but larger size, double frame, very much stronger construction, 51 in. long........... 7.50

MECHANICAL MONOPLANES. No. 805.

MADE OF TIN

Hung by a cord from ceiling they circle about the room

8 in. long.....25c.   12 in. long......50c.   16 in. long......$1.0

**A 819-93 SKYDIVER JET PLANE AND TRAC-
TOR**.....................**15.95**
Up into the clouds streaks Skydiver Jet, electric
jet motor screaming, as Skydiver prepares to
bail out, shroud lines and parachute tucked
behind him. Then it's release canopy, as Diver is
ejected high into the air, to float gently down
beneath colorful silk parachute. Giant 31" Jet
in high-impact plastic, held by youngster while
in "flight," is pulled along
on ground by powerful
7" battery-operated Trac-
tor included. Less batteries
(see below). Ship. wt.
5 lbs.
802-19 Battery Set.....**.80**

B 818-20 PILOT TRAINER (Import) **12.00**
This remarkable toy will fascinate young
(and maybe not-so-young) airline pilots.
A five-step ground-to-air procedure is fol-
lowed. "Pilot" first starts the two inboard
engines, then the outboard engines, "revs
up," and then the runway is actually moving beneath him. As he pulls back on the
wheel the 10" long airliner rises into the
air, its wheels automatically retracting into
the fuselage. To "land" the procedure is
reversed. 9" x 6" base is of durable plastic,
airliner of lithographed metal. Operates
on flashlight batteries incl. Ship. wt. 4 lbs.

C 804-092   TRU JET STREAK **4.95**
(9 yrs. up)—Motor is quickly charged from harmless, non-inflammable compressed gas for take-offs
and soaring flights. 18½″ high-impact plastic fuselage with soft nose cone. Complete with can of jet-
power gas for 100 flights. Ship. wt. 2 lbs.
818-040   EXTRA CAN OF JET GAS Jet power for above, for 100 flights. Ship. wt. 1 lb.   **1.50**

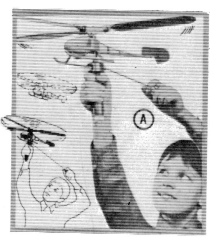

A 818-091   HELICOPTER (Import) **4.95**
A steady favorite, this dependable 9″ helicopter is exceptionally well-made. Made of light but
extremely durable plastic, it makes flights up to 100 feet. One firm quick pull on the spinner
launches it on its journey, propelled by its three big blades. Very simple to use. Ship. wt. 2 lbs.

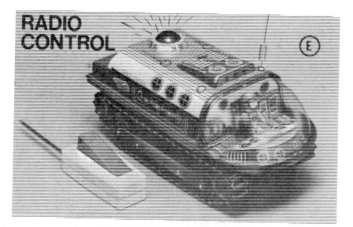

E 819-033   RADIO CONTROL SPACE PATROL **39.95**
Battery-powered ready-to-run long space patrol car is controlled from hand-held transmitter, enabling
the young driver to control car via radio signals. Push the button of transmitter and car will start and
move forward, another radio signal will change the direction to either right or left. Easy to maneuver
into all directions. 13½″ vehicle is made from strong metal, attractively styled and decorated. Red
flashing light indicates change of direction. Batteries included (import). Ship. wt. 6 lbs.

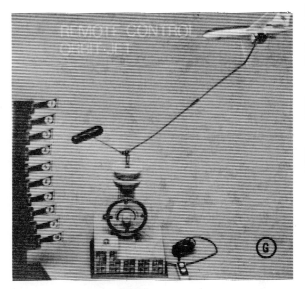

G 819-026 ORBIT JET (Import) **16.95**
(6 yrs. up)—There is tremendous fun in controlling the sleek jet
liner at different heights—forward and back. With a little more skill
the young pilot can knock over with his plane's wing tips the numbered signs on the separate tower, skillfully avoiding accidents and
crashes. Orbit jet control tower has built-in timer for additional
flying fun. Complete with batteries. Ship. wt. 5 lbs.

H 818-049 MINI ROCKET **4.95**
(9 yrs. up)—Ready-to-fly rocket blasts off into space up to heights
of 300 feet. When rocket reaches apogee of its trajectory, it noses
over gracefully and heads back to earth for a featherweight landing
on its soft nose cone. The carefully engineered Mini Rocket is propelled by harmless non-inflammable compressed gas. Can of gas
included provides approximately 25 flights. Complete with landing
stand. Ship. wt. 3 lbs.
818-110 EXTRA CAN OF GAS FOR ABOVE. **1.30**

D 818-011 APOLLO LUNAR SPACECRAFT KIT **6.95**
(9 yrs. up)—Precisely scaled at 1/70 from authentic drawings and information. Precision molded
plastic parts go easily together to build the model of this famous spacecraft which landed on the moon
in July, 1969. Kit includes all parts to build Apollo Lunar spacecraft and separate command module.
Comprehensive instructions facilitate assembly. Complete with cement. Ship. wt. 2 lbs.

Sports & games

Most children's sports are either scaled-down versions of the games adults play or ingenious variations of them. Ten-year-olds have always tried to obey the same rules in football as their big brothers at college. The gear offered in 1924 for youngsters would have been fine for the Notre Dame team if the size were right. The hockey equipment of 1931 came in sizes that fit the under-ten set but it bore the stamp of approval of a champion, Billy Mclean, who considered them great. While few tykes of three made it around the eighteen holes, the golf clubs available for them in 1923 would have satisfied any pro the right size to put them to proper use. Manufacturers of croquet sets offered vari-sized handles for the mallets to enable children to have the same advantage as their elders in family competitions.

Sports have changed subtly through the years. There is more tennis and golf played by adults and less amateur baseball. Ping-pong and billiards, even when called table tennis and pool, vary little from the 1930s until today. Polo was once covered on the sports pages of the daily newspapers. Today it is of interest to a much more exclusive group. In the 1920s, polo mallets for children who wanted to play the game on their bikes were popular, although one wonders if that would appeal to anyone now. In the 1930s when jai alai was being promoted as the coming national sport, "HI-LI" baskets were offered to forward-thinking kids, but only Floridians have retained an enthusiasm for the game. Archery is not considered a safe gift by parents now, but winter sports are taken more seriously.

Comparing sleds of the twenties with those of today proves how much more speed-oriented people are now. There were toboggans and racers then as now, but today it is very rare to find the typical sleds of the 1920s designed for smaller children. These invariably had protective railings and were meant to be used by riders who sat rather than lay on their sleds. Ideally they were to be pulled by a doting guardian.

Professional........................	Each	...5.
National Ass'n Jr............. }	in	...75
Official Nat'l League Jr.... }	Box	...$1.0
National Ass'n.............		...1.0
Official Nat'l League......		...1.2
Double Seam League Ball. }		...1.2

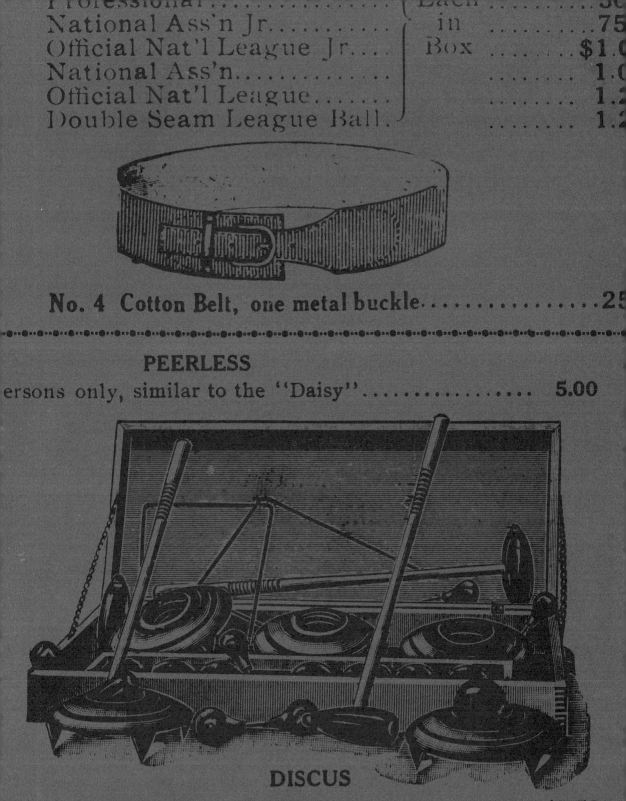

No. 4 Cotton Belt, one metal buckle................25

PEERLESS

ersons only, similar to the "Daisy".................. 5.00

DISCUS

A very interesting Lawn Game, similar to croquet, **$7.50**

GENUINE ENGLISH BOXWOOD CROQUET

We also carry a carefully selected Line of Genuine English Boxwood Croquet, both for 4 as well as for 8 players. Would be pleased to give full particulars concerning same upon request.

1912

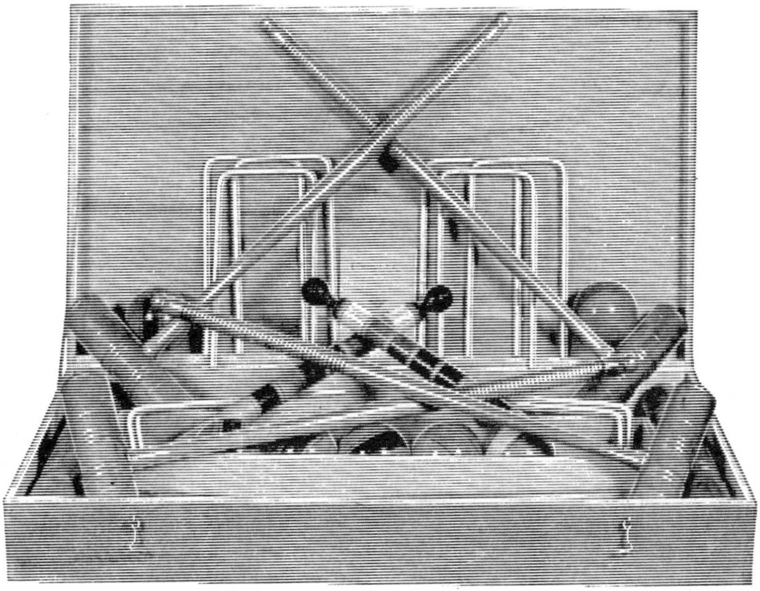

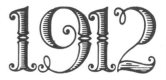

BOXWOOD CROQUET

No. 889

American Boxwood set for 8 players, 4 handles, each 18 in. and 27 in. long. Balls regulation size, heavy wire wickets painted white. A splendid set for critical players.................................. $12.00

No. X D. D.

Turkish Boxwood set, also for 8 players, same size handles as above, mallet heads 8 x 2½ in. The stock has been specially selected and well seasoned.. 24.00

THE DAISY

One of the best sets ever made of dogwood or boxwood. Large, fancy turned 7-in. mallet, painted with colors that will not fade. Short handles, tournament wickets and sockets. Fine whitewood box.. 8.00

CHILD'S BOXWOOD CROQUET SET

Made of good quality boxwood, light weight to suit children. For 4 players. Mallets and stakes nicely striped and polished............. $5.50

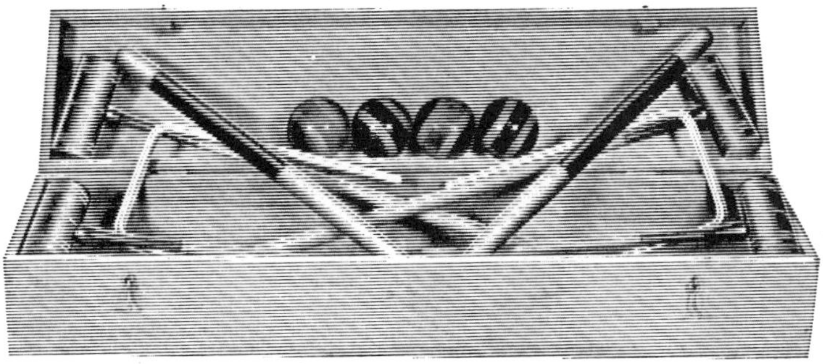

SAND BOATS (to draw)

No. 40/315. Finely painted tin, with wooden mast and muslin sail.

Hull, 10 in. long.................................. **$1.25**
    " 16 "   " **2.00**
    " 19 "   " **2.50**

FOLDING CHAIR

Trimmed with wood sand moulds, etc.... ......Price **$3.50**
Toys arranged to suit either Boys or Girls

GARDEN TOOL BASKET

Very unique combination, very fine quality basket, 8 x 12 inches, complete (like cut)................................. **$3.00**

WOODEN WHEELBARROW

With garden tools and other implements required for planting (like cut)... **$4.00**
Size of Barrow: 34 in. Shaft, 10 in. Wheel

KINDERGARTEN OUTFITS

No. 4290—Work and Play, a large assortment of occupations such as sewing, weaving, beadwork, basket work, etc., very attractive $3.50
No. 3289—Play and Work, a smaller set 1.50

PLAITING WORK

No. 3318—Weaving and painting $1.00
No. 3216—Fairy pictures plaiting 1.00

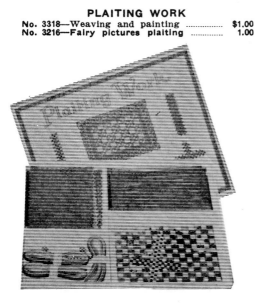

FLOWER MAKING SETS

To make a large assortment of flowers in most natural style.
No. 1521, $1.75; No. 1522, larger $2.50
No. 1523—Most complete outfit 5.00

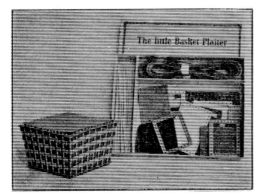

BASKET MAKER

Consisting of a variety of cardboard, bottoms and rims, wooden sticks, straw tape of various colors or beads to make useful little baskets.
No. 1134—Gold basket worker $1.00
No. 3299—The bead basket worker 2.00
No. 1154—Basket making with pearls 1.50
No. 3282—The new bead basket work........ 1.50
No. 3313—Little basket plaiter (with beads) 3.00
No. 3184—Basket making 2.50
No. 4682—Basket making (plaiting and beads) 4.50

BICYCLE POLO MALLETS

Regulation mallets of red malacca, leather bound handles, stiff medium or whippy shafts ....each **$3.00**

FIELD HOCKEY STICKS

These sticks are all imported and made of the best straight grain ash. The better sticks have from four to eight piece handles, all come in assorted weights from 18 to 24 ounces.

No. Junior — Full whipped handles ....each **$4.00**

No. Champ.—Full whipped 4 piece handle ....each **4.50**

No. 350/6—Full whipped 6 piece handle bulger model, ...each **6.50**

No. 350/7—Full whipped and taped 8 piece handle bulger model ....each **7.50**

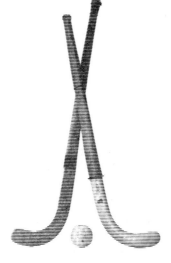

GOLF SETS

The clubs in these sets are made with the same expert skill and care that is put into the adults models. The shafts are made of hickory, the heads of steel, and grips of genuine leather. Each set includes a plaid bag, leather trimmed, three clubs and two suitable balls.

Midget Set (for ages 3 to 5) ....set **$5.00**
Junior Set (for ages 6 to 8) ....set **6.75**

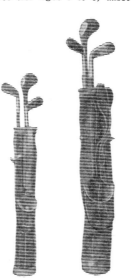

JUVENILE GOLF CLUBS AND BAGS

These clubs are modeled after the best of regulation size clubs. Great care is given to the assembling of these clubs as well as in the selection of straight grain hickory for the shafts and best quality grips.

Putters shafts 28 to 31 inches, each **$1.75**
Mashies shafts 30 to 33 inches, each **1.75**
Mid Irons shafts 31 to 35 inches, ...each **1.75**
Brassies shafts 35 to 38 inches, ...each **2.00**
Drivers shafts 35 to 38 inches, each **2.00**

The following bags made especially for Juvenile use are all leather trimmed well sewed and of stout material.

Tan canvas, brown trim ....each **$4.00**
White canvas, brown trim ....each **4.00**
Olive Green Cloth, brown trim, each **4.50**
Plaid cloth, brown trim ....each **3.00**

Juvenile Mid Iron

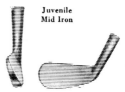

Juvenile Driver or Brassie.

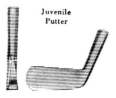

Juvenile Putter

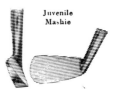

Juvenile Mashie

DOUBLE RUNNER BOB

Each sled on this Bob is made of hardwood, jointed and metal braced in a manner to give maximum strength and minimum weight. It is equipped with side rails, brakes and heavy webbing for steering. Dimensions are: extreme width 24 inches, height 10 inches, length 9½ feet, capacity 6 ....each $50.00

TOBOGGAN CUSHIONS

Regular Cushion. Filled with cotton felt, 2-inch box, extra heavy, khaki drill cover, metal tufting buttons, ties for fastening to toboggan.

3½ ft. for 5 ft. toboggan ....each $3.50
4½ ft. for 6 ft. toboggan ....each 4.50
5½ ft. for 7 ft. toboggan ....each 5.50
6½ ft. for 8 ft. toboggan ....each 6.50
7½ ft. for 9 ft. toboggan ....each 7.50

SKI BOBS

The construction of **Ski Bobs** is such that by moving the steering arm the skis may be tilted on either edge and so control direction of the bob.

A4—4 ft. long, 6 in. high, 10 in. wide .... $ 7.50
A6—6 ft. long, 6 in. high, 11 in. wide 13.50

GUARD SLEDS

No. 382—Finished in red .... $ 7.50
No. 381—Finished in white 10.00
Both 33 inches long.

BABY SLEIGH

No. 1—Finished in assorted colors, upholstered throughout $20.00

No. 385—An official Intercollegiate Football, recognized and accepted as the standard for the United States. It is made by the manufacturer who supplies the Army and Navy, many colleges, and public schools. All possible stretch removed from leather, sewed on lock-stitch machine with heavy wax thread, packed complete with lace, needle and best quality bladder..................each $10.00

No. RCS—Official Football in size and shape. Made of selected English stock, well sewed. Packed complete with needle, lace and bladder...............each 6.75

FOOTBALL JERSEYS

No. K—Made of best quality yarn, medium weight, sizes 24 to 36 inch chest; colors plain navy, maroon or black ....each $4.00
Also navy or maroon with white stripe or black with orange stripe...............each 4.50

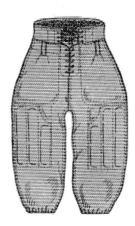

No. 4
FOOTBALL PANTS

No. 4—Best quality 8-ounce olive color duck, grey felt kidney pads, duck covered, hips well quilted, three-piece flat fibre thigh guards, sizes 28 to 32 waist measure.
Boys' ....pair $5.00
Men's ....pair 5.50
No. 3½—Made of heavy olive drab canvas, inside hip and knee pads, reeded thighs.
Boys', sizes 26 to 32.................pair 3.00
Men's ....pair 3.50

FOOTBALL BLADDERS

No. 5R—Pure gum, heavy weight, full size ....each $1.00
No. 4RP—Standard weight, junior size, ...each .65

FOOTBALL SHOES

No. F1—Good quality grain leather, waterproof soles, oak cleats, attached to steel inner sole, ankle guards, special kicking last. Sizes 1 boys' to 9 men's..pair $6.50
No. SL—Rawhide Shoe Laces, 72 inch ....pair .25

No. 217 HOSE
STOCKINGS

These footless stockings may be worn over any other stockings or socks. Colors plain or with three-inch calf stripe, colors to match Jerseys. Sizes boys' 7 to men's 10½.
No. 214—Heavy cotton........pair $1.00
No. 217—Cotton and wool, ...pair 1.50
No. 91—White cotton socks, ...pair .25

No. 2SG

SHOULDER GUARDS

No. 17 — A special Boys' Shoulder Guard. Made of white wood felt and sole leather collar bone and shoulder reinforcements, ...pair $3.50

No. 2SG — Another Boys' number, laced, reinforced felt and leather............pair 2.50

No. 5SG—Full size shoulder guard, extra white wool felt padding, moulded sole leather reinforcements, ...pair 6.00

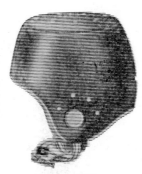

No. 2HG

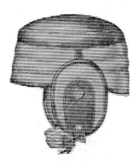

No. 1HG

HEAD HELMETS
(Mention Hat Size When Ordering)

No. 2HG—Two-piece all black leather, white felt padding, adjustable chin straps and deep cut crown............each $3.00

No. 1HG — Black crown, strong drill sides, well padded and ventilated; each $2.00

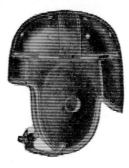

No. 6HG

No. 3HG

HEAD HELMETS
(Mention Hat Size When Ordering)

No. 6HG—Best quality black leather moulded to shape, heavy perforated felt padding, adjustable head band and chin straps............each $7.50

No. 3HG—Made of selected black cowhide, ventilating holes through padding and leather, adjustable head band and chin strap......each $5.00

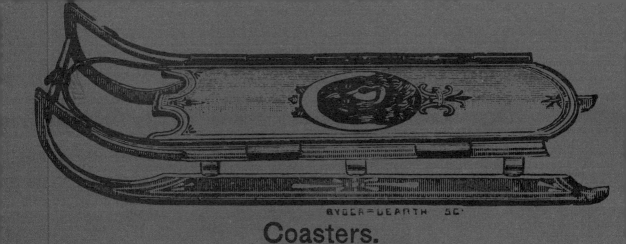

Coasters.

With flat and round steel runners, $1.00, $1.50, $1.75, $2.00, $2.25
$4.00, $4.50, $5.00

Boys' Sleds.

A large assortment of strong and pretty Sleds, varnished on the wood or
painted........$1.00, $1.50, $1.75, $2.25 (see cut), $3.00, $3.50, $4.50

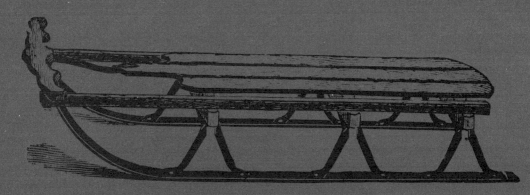

Flexible Flyer.

A new invention in Coasters, with patent steering gear, entirely made of ste
$2.25, $3.50, $4.00, $5

SPORT SKATES

No brakes—but who cares? These tricky sport skates hold a lot of fun in store for lucky youngsters with shoe sizes from 2 up. Rubber-tired, roller-bearing wheels scoot the pilot along at a thrilling, but safe speed. Pair..........$5.50

SCOOTER SKATE

One foot off, and one foot on. And away you go! The scooter skate rolls along on three rubber-tired wheels. It's easy to operate. Shoe plate adjustable from 8 to 11 inches $1.25

KANGRU—SPRINGSHU—Fun for all

The two steel coils enable the youngsters to jump easily or run with extra spring to every step. Metal foot plates with straps, bottoms have rubber surfaces. 4 sizes to accommodate.
30 to 45 lbs.; 45 to 60 lbs.; 60 to 75 lbs.; 75 to 100 lbs.
Pair $3.00

BOBBY McLEAN ICE SKATES

Bobby McLean's Ladies Championship Hockey Outfit. Shoe made of two tone brown and tan selected leather, fleece lined 8 inches high, attached to a special chromium plated tubular skate. Sizes 4 to 9...$15.00

Bobby McLean's Championship hard toe hockey Outfit. The shoe has black calf uppers, trimmed in brown, lined throughout, attached to chromium plated tubular skate. Sizes 5 to 10...$16.50

Bobby McLean's Championship soft toe outfit, otherwise like hard toe outfit. Sizes 3 to 12...$15.00

No. 20—Boys' skate and shoe outfit, black shoe, strap and buckle. Inside reinforcement. Sizes from children's 9 to adult's 8. Pair.............................$9.00

No. 35—Girls' skate and shoe outfit, shoe 1" higher, lined; otherwise like No.20. Pair $10.00

SLED SKATES

For very small children, too young to use single runner skates. Strap heel and toe. Adjustable. Nickle-plated. Pair...$0.85

SNOW SKATES

Buddy Snow Skates can be used on crusted snow or ice. Made to fit all size shoes, fastened with raw hide lace. Pair...$1.75

HOCKEY STICKS

HOCKEY PUCK

SLED SKATES

Bobby McLean ICE SKATES

SNOW SKATES

HOCKEY STICKS

All hockey sticks are made of the finest grade selected rock elm.
Junior ....$0.50   Crackshot $0.65
Minnesota 1.25

HOCKEY PUCKS

No. H.P.—Best rubber, official size and weight; fresh and lively.................$0.50

SNOW BIKE

Two wide steel runners, 22" long, support wooden platform on which rider can be comfortably seated with feet on foot rest, steering with wide handlebars. Equipped with hand brake...$6.50

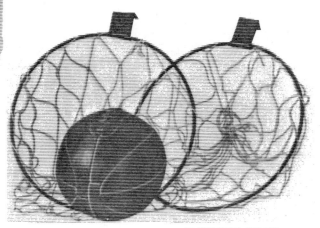

No. T-22 — Junior Rockne Helmet. Made of special tanned strap leather, tan color, lined throughout with white felt, moulded crown reinforced with six leather bands. Has inner web suspension to absorb shock, moulded ear pieces and elastic adjustment.....**$3.75**

No. T-23—Junior Rockne Shoulder Pads, made of white felt, covered with tan grain leather, moulded fibre shoulder caps and collar bone protector; round elastic under arm, laces front and back **$3.25**

No. T-18—Junior Rockne ready laces valve type **football,** made of genuine full grain cowhide, pebbled; canvas lined, regulation size **$5.00**

No. T-24—Junior Rockne Football Pants. Built of heavy tan duck, white felt hip and kidney pads, flexible fibre-reinforcement at top, curved fibre thigh guards, leather knee patch and laced front. Sizes 26 to 34. Pair....**$5.00**

No. T-201/3—Junior Rockne Footless Football **stockings,** can be worn over any others. Wool and cotton mixture. Blue with gold stripe. Pair............**$1.25**

No. T-115/3—Junior Jersey, made of medium weight good quality pure worsted yarn. Navy blue with gold stripes. Sizes 26 to 34..................**$3.00**

BASKETBALL GOALS

No. T-100—Light-weight regulation size goal with flat iron ring and net, special bracket which can be secured to any post. Each........................**$1.75**
Pair 3.50

No. T-102—Official goals' with strong rigid ring supported at three points by bracket and two arms, heavy cord nets, each **$2.75**
Pair 5.50

101

GOOD OLD GAMES

EVERYBODY PLAYS

Shovelboard, Basket Ball, Croquet, Billiards, Golf, Bowling, good for an entire Evening's Sport, Price of entire set..............................$1.00

wl 8¼ ½ in. $1.50

65 FINE GAMES ON

CROWN COMBINATIO GAME BOARD.

Trade Mark.

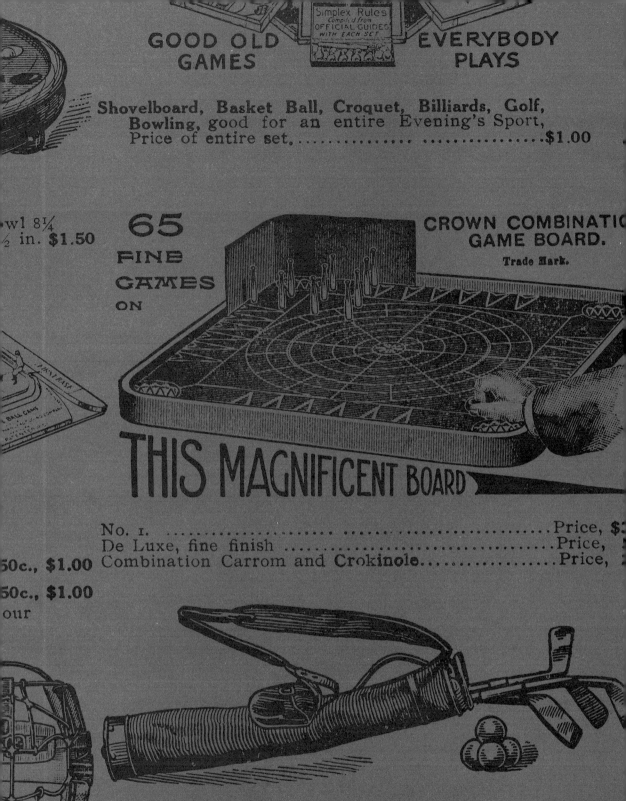

THIS MAGNIFICENT BOARD

No. 1...Price, $
De Luxe, fine finish................................Price,
50c., $1.00 Combination Carrom and Crokinole................Price,

50c., $1.00
our

CHILDREN'S GOLF

These Clubs are made of the very best material and are known under the name "Clan"

Iron clubs, Putter, Lofter, Cleek, 24 in., 27 in., 30 in. shaft
Wooden Clubs, Driver, Brassie, 24 in., 27 in., 30 in., 33 in, 36 in., shaft..............................Price $1.50 Each
Children's Golf Bags, white canvas, leather trimmed 27 inches..$2.50
ask....50c. Remade Balls...25c. Each
teur $1.00 Prices of Standard Balls on request.

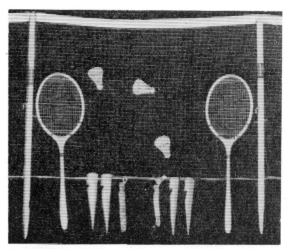

No. 23/705—A low priced set consisting of 2 "Star" Racquets, Net and 2 Shuttlecocks, book of rules. **$7.50**

No. 23/706—**Highgrade Set** with 2 "Scout" Racquets, 18 x 2½ feet Net, 6 Shuttlecocks, 1 inch Posts and Badminton Guide. **$14.50**

Hi Li Game—Children as well as adults will be fascinated with this game of Hi Li adapted from the Cuban. The rules were simplified to make a more enjoyable game out of it. The rubber ball is thrown and caught with the reed basket. Not quite as simple as it looks, however, plenty of fun and healthy exercise is assured. Can be played in either large or small space, no set boundaries are necessary. Complete with 2 baskets and 1 ball.

No. 23/693—For children 8 - 14 years. **$3.50**
No. 23/643—For adults. **5.00**

Archery Sets—Handsome sets complete with wooden stands 4½ feet high with brightly marked leatherette-covered straw targets.

No. 32/8—Stand, 18-inch target, 4-ft. lemon-wood bow, four regulation metal tipped arrows, and leather quiver. Complete **$6.50**

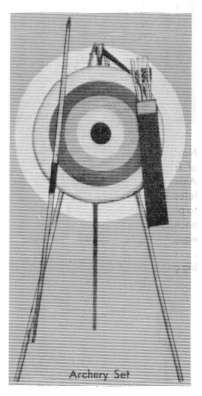

Archery Set

Ping Pong Table and Equipment

No. 23/260—(Illustrated) **Ping Pong Set** including 4 rubber faced racquets with wood handles, 12 balls, 66 inch net and heavy posts and Ping Pong Manual. **$5.00**

No. 23/347—**Table Tennis Set** with 4 full sized 3-ply Bats (2 sanded, 2 rubber faced), 4 Balls, 66 inch Net and extension brackets. **$3.75**

No. 23/348—**Table Tennis Set** with 4 full sized rubber faced 5-ply Bats with wooden handles, 8 Balls, 66 inch metal bound net and fine adjustable brackets. **$6.75**

No. 23/349—**Table Tennis, 3-ply Bat,** rubber faced. . **1.00**

No. 23/350—**Table Tennis, 5-ply Bat,** rubber faced. . **1.50**

No. 23/12—**Ping Pong Balls,** each . . . . **.15**

No. 40/92—**Official Ping Pong Table,** tournament size 5 x 9 feet, with 5-ply wooden top, giving a fast, hard playing surface. Hinged in center with folding legs and strong metal braces. Painted green with white lines. (Racquets, Balls and Net not included). **$22.50**

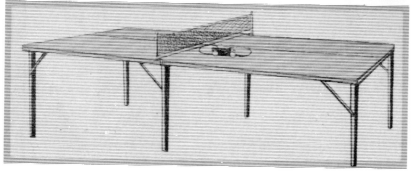

No. 23/618—**Pigskin Football Game**—A scientific board game of football invented by Lieut. Tom Hamilton, head coach at Annapolis. It is real football and will bring you up-to-date on latest rules, but one does not have to be familiar with the game to play and enjoy it. Cards control the moves of the two teams, each player using a full team and substitutes. Included with the equipment is a pad of charts to record every detail of the play . . . also for use when following actual radio broadcasts of the big games. **$2.50**

No. 23/293—Sky Shoot Players use a harmless repeating rifle shooting rubber bands to hit a target. When this target is hit, it releases a parachute high into the air, which, when falling, may be shot at with the repeating rifle. Complete with a parachute, target, rifle and rubber bands....... **$1.00**

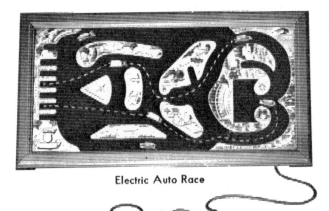

Electric Auto Race

No. 23/152—Electric Auto Race A new idea, beautifully designed in 6 colors. Six tiny automobiles are started and by connecting the 8 feet of cord including switch to the house current the jet black metal surface vibrates and moves the cars in all directions. There are obstacles and penalties and, of course, the first car entering the "finish" line wins the race. Every car has an even chance, and not until the finish is one able to tell the winner. Works on **A.C. house current only**.................. **$3.00**

Home Pool Tables—They are modern in design, have distinctive features and are rigidly braced. The finish is "Cape Cod" maple and the bed is covered with soft-on-the-eye cloth. The "Roll-A-Way" feature returns ball to tray. Complete with full playing equipment and book of rules.
No. 42/38—Size 50 x 27½ x 29" high...................... **$12.75**
No. 42/40—Size: 60 x 31½ x 30" high...................... **$19.75**
No. 42/41—Size: 66 x 35 x 31" high...................... **$30.00**

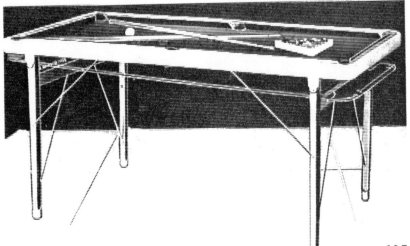

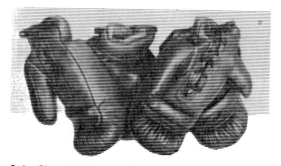

Boxing Gloves—Well made professional-type leather gloves, correct in every detail. Made of extra fine selection of glove leather. Well padded.

No. 7 – 7—Sizes: 3-5 years. Set of 4 Gloves. **$3.95**
No. 7 – 8—Sizes: 5-7 years. Set of 4 Gloves. 4.60
No. 7 – 9—Sizes: 7-10 years. Set of 4 Gloves. 5.25
No. 7 – 10—Sizes: 10-12 years. Set of 4 Gloves. 6.00
No. 7 – 11—Sizes: 12-14 years. Set of 4 Gloves. 6.95

No. 7 – 39—Floor Punching Bag—Good, durable quality genuine leather, an excellent exerciser for the boy, developing shoulder and arm muscles and cultivating alertness. Mounted on sturdy wood cross stand, works on strong spring set into rubber base which brings back the bag sharply as soon as it's struck. Height 40". Complete. . **$5.75**

No. 7 – 33—Busy Kiddie Gym—A specially constructed complete gym, swing, trapeze and rings, that takes up little more than doorway space in the playroom! The doorway clamp is the feature—heavy steel but finished with rubber tubes for woodwork protection—absolutely safe. Swing seat suspended on 76" adjustable ropes. Very substantial. **$9.75**

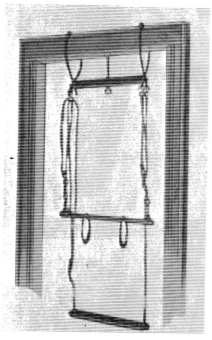

No. 7 – 102—Overhead Punching Bag—An invaluable outfit for muscular development and coordination as well as timing of punches for the boxer. The professional size striking bag is made of 2-tone smooth leather reinforced with strong canvas lining. Has a valve type bladder and swivel hanger. The steel ring platform, 22" in diameter, comes with strong wooden braces. **$6.95**

No. 8 – 13—Treasure Belt—A handsome, light tan, genuine Cowhide belt with richly studded and embossed designs. Full 3" wide with 3 snap pockets, one containing an efficient 5-POWER TELESCOPE, another a FLAT FLASHLIGHT, and the other an accurate COMPASS and the biggest surprise of all—a PERISCOPE RING—a ring small enough to wear on the finger, yet the mounting has an ingenious periscope device. Sizes 24 to 34. BE SURE TO STATE SIZE. EXCLUSIXE WITH F. A. O. SCHWARZ. **$5.90**

"Swim-Fins"—Swimming like a fish becomes a reality with these swim aids. Practically double the speed, double the fun and only half the effort. Developed by Owen Churchill, international Olympic swimmer, from crude fins used by the world renowned Tahitian surfmen. Simply slip on the foot, strap over the heel and mark your time! You can easily understand their speed-strength from the fish-like fin design. Imagine doubling your speed, and you will, with the aid of "Swim-Fins." Durable quality black rubber in all sizes.

No. 7 – 67—For shoe size 3-5 . . . . **$7.50**

No. 7 – 68—For shoe size 5-7 . . . . 7.50

No. 7 – 69—For shoe size 7-9 . . . . 7.50

No. 7 – 73—For shoe size 10-11 . . . . 7.50

No. 7 – 70—For shoe size 12-14 . . . . 7.50

No. 6 – 59—Wood Sand Pail and Tools—A 7" pail that will not rust is an advantage . . . hence this wooden pail. The 6-piece wooden sand tool set is an ideal companion and consists of hoe, rake, 2 shovels, pounder, and mold. Complete. **$2.00**

No. 7 – 81—"Sea-Dive" Mask—Protection to both the eyes and nose while exploring under water. The one-piece rubber mask molds itself tightly to the face excluding all water and permits full view through heavy glass window, 5" in diameter. A heavy elastic band, adjustable, with rust-proof buckle, holds it on head. **$2.75**

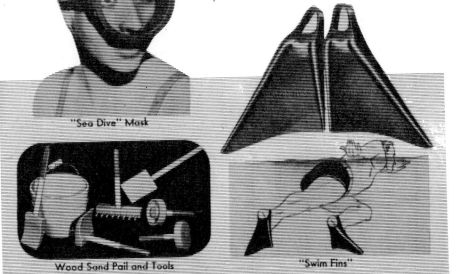

"Sea Dive" Mask

Wood Sand Pail and Tools

"Swim Fins"

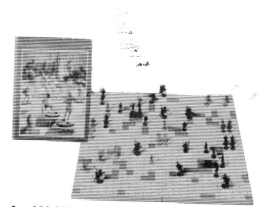

L 823-233 FEUDAL Ship. wt. 3 lbs. . . . **8.95**
An exciting medieval war game, combining military
strategy with chess-like moves. With colorful playing
board, divided screen, playing pieces and instructions.
For 2 to 6 players. Average playing time is 1 hour.

A 823-013 3-D CHESS **12.00**
A space-age concept of one of history's favorite games.
Chess in three dimensions. No change in chess rules,
only the dimension of depth added. Easy to play and
exciting, too. Gracefully curved tree and square base
are finished in glossy black. The three playing levels
are transparent and permanently etched with attractive
chess board design. With playing rules. Ship. wt. 4 lbs.

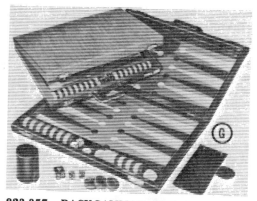

823-357 BACKGAMMON SET **19.95**
15" x 10½" x 2¼" closed. 1¼" men. Ship. wt. 5 lbs.
823-360 BACKGAMMON SET **25.95**
18½" x 12" x 2" closed. 1½" men. Ship. wt. 7 lbs.

H 823-016 GAME OF GO **10.00**
(10 yrs. up)—Originating in China 4000 years ago, Go
has retained its popularity through the centuries. Players alternately place one stone at a time on 18" x 18"
board grid. For 2 players. Ship. wt. 5 lbs.

J 823-161 TRIPOLEY (KING EDITION) **6.95**
(10 yrs. up)—All the thrills and suspense of three
great card games—Hearts, Poker and Michigan Rum-
my. A deluxe green vinyl layout, padded with soft
foam, with Tripoley layout in gold and red. 42" x 27".
Cards and chips included. Ship. wt. 3 lbs.

SOAP BUBBLE SETS

...aking soap bubbles, tin pipe and soap.....................25c.
..le set with racket..50c.
..box with 2 basins, straws, pipes, etc........................$1.00

SHOOTS OVER 25 FEET

IT SHOOTS,—
YOU CATCH.

This is where you work the Gun

25¢

ALL NEW YORK AMUSES ITSELF PLAYING

KAN·U·KATCH

25c. Each, 50c. Per Pair

COPPER JACK STONES

Set of 5..3c.
Jack Stone Balls......................................1c.

No. 9059

MARBLES

We carry a large assortment of Glass, Porcelain and real Agate Marbles. Prices according to size and quality from
1c. to 30c. per dozen

Marbles in bags, many different kinds, felt bag, 25c.
Chamois bag. 50c.

CUP AND

BALL

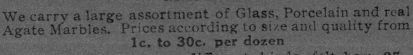

COMP

The object is to hurl the ball in the air and catch it in the cup.
..n. long..25c.   9 in. long..35c.   10½ in. long..50c.   12 in. long..65c.

Metal

JUMPING ROPES

Sets of
..rnished handles, white rope ....20c.   Sets of
..ncy painted handles, better rope.............25c., 50c.   Sets of
                                                              Sets of

Costumes & uniforms

Play uniforms did not become popular until after 1900. Earlier, some children had ball costumes that they might have been able to use for play if they did not get caught. These might be more complex than the soldier, cowboy, and policeman outfits that have satisfied children's needs since the beginning of the century. The 1911 uniforms and costumes are in the same spirit as those made today, but neither policemen nor soldiers dress the same now as then. The boy of 1911 had to have the patience to wind leggings around his legs if he wanted to be a convincing soldier. Uniforms were mass-produced as playclothes. These were ordinarily worn over everyday clothes but some could substitute for them since they were hardy enough to withstand the rigors of battle. The differences between boys and girls was emphasized in the play uniforms they wore. The neatest thing available for a boy was a doctor's suit since he was supposed to insist on the rough and tumble. Girls were to revel in lovely gowns. The choice was Fairy Queen one year and Fairy Princess the next. They could also be Spanish ladies of mystery or sinister Gypsy-like types with tambourines. It took something of a battle to find a cowgirl or nurse's outfit that might be useful in an active game.

Costumes reflected both political and cultural events. Peace inspired one kind of uniform, war another. A popular movie or comic strip might make pirates more or less important. The Second World War Air Raid Warden outfits suggested that men and women had similar challenges, but those for the Red Cross nurses were extravagantly feminine. Although children today are less concerned with clothing, uniforms still have a great appeal since they make the world of make-believe more convincing. Those who like to go all the way have found disguise and make-up kits useful and a way of identifying even more strongly with some of the heroes and heroines who are known best as movie and television characters.

POLICEMAN OUTFIT

Blue Coat, trousers, hand-cuff, cap, belt, club and pistol. $3.00

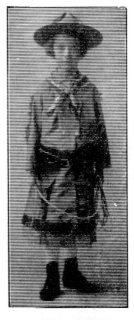

INDIAN CHIEF SUIT

Khaki cloth, with red and yellow fringe.........$2.50
With leather fringe, best quality...............**5.00**

MILITARY SUIT

Regulation Army Khaki Coat, trousers, leggings and cap.........**$3.00**

COW GIRL OUTFIT

Consisting of blouse, skirt, hat, lariat and pistol case with belt... ..... **$4.00**

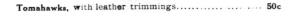

Tomahawks, with leather trimmings............. .... 50c

FIREMAN'S SUIT

Consisting of blue trousers, red shirt and cap.....**$3.00**

SCOUT SUIT
Regulation Army Khaki coat, trousers, leggings, cap and haversack.............$6.00

INDIAN SQUAW SUIT
Khaki cloth, with red and yellow fringe.......$2.50
With leather fringe, best quality 5.00

These Suits are made of fast color material, well sewn and of correct design and cut. If desired they may be worn over the ordinary clothes. Boys and girls will highly appreciate them.

To insure proper fitting patrons are requested, when ordering uniforms to state number or size of clothing ordinarily worn by the child.

INDIAN WIGWAMS

Made of Waterproof Tan color Duck with Indian characters painted on sides.
No. 5. 6 feet high, 16 feet in circumference, including
    5 Jointed Poles.   Price............ ......$6.00
No. 6. 8 feet high, 27 feet in circumference, including
    6 Jointed Poles.   Price........... ...... 10.00
Leather Quivers with Arrows........................1.25, 2.25
Leather Moccasins, all sizes, ranging in price from 75c. to 1.75

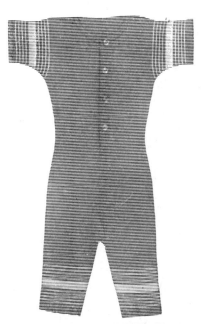

OYS' TWO-PIECE SUITS— TRIMMED

201W. Made of medium weight orsted. Trimmed. Shirts sleeveless. olors—Navy blue trimmed in white, avy blue trimmed in red, Heather mix re trimmed in red, Oxford trimmed in ale blue. Sizes 26 to 34. .Price **$3.00**

301. Made of heavy weight worsted. rimmed. Shirts sleeveless. Colors— avy blue trimmed in red, Navy blue rimmed in white, Heather mixture rimmed in red, Oxford trimmed in red. izes 26 to 34. . . . . .Price **$2.50**

300. Same as No. 301, in plain colors nly. Colors—Navy blue, black or Ox rd. Sizes 26 to 34. . . . . . .Price **$2.50**
Notice—Extra sizes in all styles.

BOYS' TWO-PIECE SUITS— SILK TRIMMED

No. 2319. Made of finest quality worsted. Full fashioned throughout. Silk trimmed. Sleeveless shirts. Colors—Navy blue trimmed in gold and black trimmed in royal blue. Sizes, ages 8 to 16 years. . . . . .Price **$5.00**

No. 2329. Same quality and style as No. 2319. Made in latest heather mixture, trimmed in red. Sizes, ages 8 to 16 years. . . . . .Price **$5.50**

No. 2306. Same quality and style as No. 2319. With a silk hair line stripe running through suit, making it a very attractive garment. Colors—Blue mixture trimmed in lavender, green heather mixture trim med in red. Sizes, ages 8 to 16 years. . . . . .Price **$6.50**

CHILDREN'S ONE-PIECE SUITS— SILK TRIMMED

No. D2329. Made of finest quality medium weight worsted. Silk trimmed. Colors—Red trimmed in white, Navy blue trimmed red or white, and Heather mixture trimmed in red. Sizes ages 2 to 10 years. . . . . .Price **$3.75**

No. D214. Made in light weight worsted, trimmed, quarter sleeves, buttons down front. Colors—Red trimmed in white, Navy trimmed in white, Navy trimmed in red, Heather mixture trimmed in red. Sizes, ages 2 to 10 years. . . . . .Price **$2.50**

No. D216. Same as No. D214, excepting this suit has a collar, making it a practical little girls' suit. Colors —Red trimmed in white, Navy blue trimmed in white. Sizes, ages 2 to 8 years. . . . . . . .Price **$2.50**

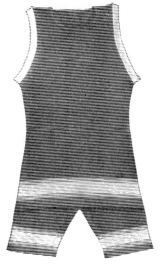

CHILDREN'S ONE-PIECE PLAIN SUITS

No. 212. Made of light weight worsted, quarter sleeves. Buttons down front. Plain colors only. Colors—Navy blue or red. Sizes, ages 2 to 10 years. . . . . .Price **$2.00**

No. D19. Made of good weight, very soft worsted. A particularly good suit for Small Children. Colors— White trimmed in baby blue, white trimmed in pink, red trimmed in white, pink trimmed in white, and baby blue trimmed in white. Sizes, ages 1 to 8 years. . . . . .Price **$3.00**

No. C. Boys' Swimming Suit, made of light weight worsted. Two buttons on shoulder strap. Colors— Navy blue only. Sizes 26 to 34. . . . . . . .Price **$3.00**

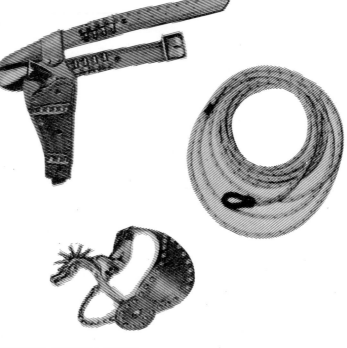

JEWELED BELT

No. 89J—Cowhide leather belt and holster studded and jeweled. Belt holds eight dummy cartridges, pistol and holster..............$3.50

No. 89—Similar to above, except without studs and jewels........ 2.50

LASSO

No. 105—Hand made of heavy ⅜in. spotted wax rope with leather Honda, 22 feet long $2.00

SPURS

No. 960—Has he won his spurs? If he's been on his good behavior, a gift of a pair of spurs will tactfully show your gratitude. These spurs have wide nickel-studded leather straps and revolving star rowel, pair $2.75

WESTERN COWBOY OUTFIT

No. 620—**Ten Gallon Cowboy Hat,** made of fine fawn colored felt, sizes 6¾ to 7⅛..$3.50

No. 268—**Colored Suede Leather Hat, Band** with leather rosette set with jewel.. $0.50

No. 500—**Colored Silk Bandana,** hempstitched edge, decorated with cowboy design 1.25

Medium Weight Flannel Plaid Shirt, collar attached, has one pocket, sizes 4 to 14 .... 2.00

Vest made of buckskin colored leather, has two pockets, decorated with horseshoe designs and red fringe. Sizes 4 to 14 .... 4.50

Cowboy Chaps made of heavy suede buckskin colored leather, trimmed with red fringe, tie strings, and nickel studs; has one pocket trimmed with horseshoe design. Sizes 4 to 14 ....10.00

No. 89J—**Jeweled Belt and Holster,** made of cowhide leather, studded and jeweled. Belt holds eight dummy cartridges, pistol and holster 3.50

No. 369—**Soft Tan Leather Cuffs,** studded with nail heads and trimmed with red leather. Horseshoe-trimmed with nails as design. Pair 1.50

The above suit, complete 25.00

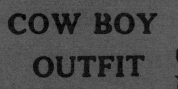

COW BOY OUTFIT

Shirt and trousers of Khaki, sombrero, lariat, leather belt and pistol case with pistol, bandana neckerchief..............$4.00

1932

OLD-FASHIONED GIRL

No. R-62—This dainty costume of flowered silk brings back the romance of crinoline days. Beneath the long-waisted bodice the ruffle-trimmed hoop skirt is gathered full. The neck is finished with a lace-edged fichu and net ruffles fall gracefully from the elbow-length sleeves. A becoming poke bonnet with long streamers and amusing lace-ruffled white pantelettes on elastic waist-band accompany the costume. Sizes: 8 to 16 years.....................................**$8.75**

CASTILIAN

No. R-60—Rich with the flavor of sunny Spain is this charming costume. The long-waisted bodice is of red satin. Black net flounces edged with gold ribbon swirl gracefully over a brilliant red underskirt with a real hoop. Gold spangle edges the neckline and the sash is of yellow satin. A golden comb, a full black lace mantilla and a romantic red rose form the head-dress. Sizes: 6 to 14 years **$8.75**

FAIRY QUEEN

No. R-16—The girl who wears this costume will be a queen in her own right. The sheen of the white rayon gown is enhanced by the silver stars dotting the flounced skirt. A single star gleams at the neck of the straight bodice. The star-studded. chiffon drapery ties to the wrists to give a wing-like effect. Belt is of silver ribbon. The white headband has a star at the front which is repeated on the magical silver wand. Sizes: 8 to 14 years. **Few costumes can compare with this in gossamer-like beauty or in quality**..................**$12.00**

CROWN

No. R-0181—Five-pointed, three-starred crown of silver, fastening at back with hooks **$2.50**

TAMBOURINE GIRL

No. R-41—Music and dancing and this tambourine girl costume for color! The dress is most becoming with its yellow organdy blouse with short puffed sleeves. The full skirt of clear, light red rayon trimmed with blue and gold ribbon has a deep band of figured rayon in rich purple, red and gold tones. The snug black velvet bodice with flat, yellow flowers, laces in front. Bead-tassels trim the neck of the dress and ornament the front of the red rayon kerchief, caught back at the neck. The dress hooks at the back. Sizes: 6 to 14 years. **An exclusive SCHWARZ creation**........................**$6.75**

SOLDIER'S DRESS UNIFORM

No. R-23—Braid and brass buttons for young "Files on parade." Includes smart blue cutaway trimmed with white braid and brass buttons, decorative epaulets, white cuffs and buckled cross belt; white trousers with blue stripe, elastic waistband style and black shako with chin strap. Sizes 4 to 14 years **$3.75**

SOLDIER SUIT

No. R-310—For marching, drilling and all kinds of real soldiering is this suit of khaki coat, trousers and cap. Cross guns on cap and leather Sam Browne belt. Sizes 4 to 14 years. Complete **$2.75**

FIREMAN SUIT

No. R-511—Fireman Suit, fast color red shirt, navy blue trousers, red helmet, with front shield, red belt and brass fastener. Sizes 2 to 14 years **$2.75**

1936

No. 23/622—**Fencing Set**—Quite the art and much fun to become adept at fencing with this harmless set. Includes two strong fiber protection plates with numbered score, two safety head masks which have wire netting and two swords of flexible reed with rubber suction cups that adhere to the numbered score plate if the player's aim is successful. Set complete for two. Suitable for Boys or Girls 6 to 14 years. **$5.00**

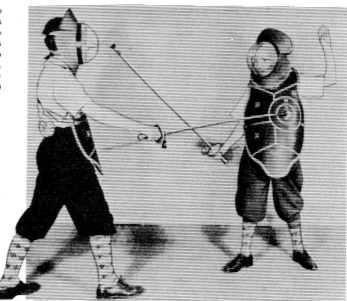

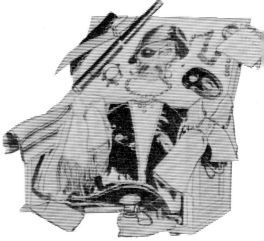

No. 8/123—**Pirate Suit**—A pirate suit bold for roistering blades who sail under the black flag. Skull and crossbones are flaunted brazenly on the black vestee. A bright red shirt and gay striped shorts with elastic waistband and a brilliant yellow fringed sash supply the color. The dashing black and red pirate hat also displays the skull and crossbones. Black puttees with red cuffs. Sizes: 4 to 14 years. BE SURE TO STATE SIZE. . . . **$4.00**

No. 8/8—**Pirate Chest**—"Yo, ho ho, look what we've here!" Equipment and plunder for the young pirate bold who would sail the Spanish Main. All in special antiqued chestnut case holed and marked as tho' it were dug from the land of hidden treasure. There's first a complete pirate's costume (for full description see No. 8/123 above), also a harmless scabbard and pistol, a most efficient 10-power micro-telescope which extends fully 32 inches for spying. Plenty of booty like bracelets, necklaces, earrings, money bag with pirate's gold, etc., and two masks for better disguise. Chest, 24 x 13 x 13 inches with hinged front and cover for easy access and two rope handles for carrying. Order by size for correct pirate suit. Sizes: 4 to 14. OUR OWN COMBINATION. **$13.75**

No. 18/43—New Disguise Kit—The popularity of our last year's combination has prompted this different assortment. Each disguise is self-attachable, no paste or adhesive necessary. There are 16 pieces in all and included are revolving eyes on eye glasses, mustaches and beards, false ears, teeth and noses, also a complete oriental make-up. OUR OWN COMBINATION in 11 x 17 inch hinged box. **$2.50**

No. 8/136—Actor's Outfit—A real theatrical make-up set including grease, paint in various shades, nose putty, tooth wax, powder. Also extra hair for side burns, whiskers, etc. A monocle for special occasions. Size 13 x 10 inches. . . . **$2.50**

No. 8/70—Wigs—Long curl mohair wig. Blond or auburn. STATE COLOR. **$1.75**

No. 8/69—Colonial style. White mohair with three side curls. **$1.75**

No. 10/142—Detective Kit—Play "G-Men" or Scotland Yard with this set. A detectaphone electrically operated by standard batteries can be concealed while the listeners some distance away secure the incriminating evidence. After which finger prints can be made with the outfit supplied of ink, pad and paper. A special Police Badge is included to make the necessary arrests possible. **$2.50**

121

No. 8 – 15—Air Raid Warden Set—There is no national standard Air Warden's Outfit but there are certain essentials and here are some for the younger aspirants—a wide white webb belt with "Air Raid Warden" imprint from which hangs a whistle, a luminous blackout button, a white leather holster containing for emergencies an all metal "Army 45" repeating revolver. Then too is an olive drab all metal helmet besides a special chest flashlight (red and white lens) with body leather straps. **$5.75**

No. 8 – 18—Military Police Set—The authority which goes with these boys plus their position of side arm is the envy of their younger compatriots so why not satisfy this ambition with this white leather belt, with its short wooden billy, leather holster containing an 8" repeating pistol, and belt loops containing 5 cartridges. To make it authentic is a brown suede cloth arm-band with the necessary **"MP"** in white. **$3.50**

No. 8 – 42—Army Officer—While the material and insignia are not official, there is enough in the brass buttons alone for Junior Military requirements. Of durable brown cotton tweed with gold braid seams down trousers. Blouse has 4 pockets with brass buttons, a service insignia, and gold stars on collar. Cap has army insignia, and there is a leather Sam Browne belt. Sizes 4 to 14 yrs. STATE SIZE. **$5.75**

No. 8 – 34—Naval Officer (With Compass and Belt)—For very safe maneuvers this naval costume comes supplied with a **Compass and Belt**. No danger of "off the course" wanderings because the dandy compass will be your guide. High ranking you'll be too, with the multiple service stripes and double insignias on the navy blue cotton twill jacket with brass "eagle" buttons. Comfortably full cut trousers with belt loops. Tan leather belt with compass. Sizes 4 to 14 years. STATE SIZE. **$5.20**

No. 8 – 38—Marine Officer—The snappiest of all regulation uniforms is the marines' dress uniform and here is the Junior Model in cotton drill having a Navy blouse with brass buttons, 4 pockets, braid on sleeve and shoulder, service ribbon, and crossed guns on lapels. The pants are lighter blue with bright red wide stripe down the seam while the cap has insignia and wide red and yellow band. This band matches the wide red and yellow belt with brass buckle. Sizes 4 to 14 years. STATE SIZE. **$6.50**

No. 8 – 33—Transport Pilot—You'll be all set to pilot for any air lines because the very necessary badge comes with detachable insignia insertions for all the different companies. Costume is authentically designed of sturdy blue denim with brass "airplane" buttons on the braid-trimmed jacket with sleeve emblem. Tan leather Sam Browne belt. Well-cut trousers with belt loops. Peaked cap to match. Sizes 4 to 14 years. STATE SIZE. **$5.00**

No. 8 – 43—Air Hostess Costume—Very "apropos" of the times when "young misses" must be just as air-minded as their brothers. Carefully copied from the authentic "airways" design with waistband skirt and neat pocketed jacket of blue cotton twill with necessary winged emblem. Matching overseas cap with brilliant braid trim and emblem. White cotton sleeveless blouse. Sizes 4 to 14 years. STATE SIZE. **$6.95**

No. 8 – 26—Doctor Outfit—"Young and aspiring Dr. Kildares" will be ever ready for emergencies in this outfit whether sister's dolly needs medical aid or should a "wounded" buddy arrive from the "front". Of durable white cotton fabric with "Blue Cross" emblem on cap and the front of the 3/4 length sleeve doctor's coat that ties at the neck in back. Elastic waist trousers. (Stethoscope not included—if wanted please refer to page 28, on which is illustrated and described **No. 9 – 86**—Little Army Doctor and Nurse Outfit $3.50.) Sizes: 6 to 14 years. STATE SIZE. **$3.95**

No. 8 –29—Nurse Outfit—A most becoming and authentic uniform without the official emblem, consisting of a white broadcloth dress, cap, apron, and a red lined blue duvetyn cape. The dress ties down the back with the customary tape ties, has a full skirt gathered at the waist, short sleeves, and a low stand-up collar. On the patch pocket of the apron and on the cap is a round red seal with a blue cross. Sizes: 6 to 14 years. STATE SIZE. **$5.95**

No. 8 – 45—Uncle Sam Costume—We're getting many calls these patriotic times for this famous costume. Exceptionally well done with navy blue cotton duvetyn "tailed" jacket, clever brass buttoned vestee of blue-and-white star-print sateen with gleaming white satin collar and red-striped bow tie. Red-and-white striped elastic-waist pants and, of course, the formal high "topper" to match. Sizes 4 to 14 years. STATE SIZE. **$6.95**

No. 8 – 36—Patriotic Costume—A colorful 2-piece silk rayon outfit. The full skirt is gathered at waist and is made of wide bands of red, white and blue; the solid blue waist, square necked and short sleeved, is trimmed with shiny silver stars. An elastic band holds the small flat hat at a jaunty angle. The hat is made of ruffled layers of red, white and blue with ribbon back streamers. Sizes 6 to 14 years. STATE SIZE. **$7.50**

No. 8 – 27—Fairy Princess—"A costume winged and airy, a costume for a very good fairy." Snowy white Rayon Satin all a-glitter with silver stars adorning the bodice, front and back, and shiny tinsel ribbon round the waist and banding the long gracefully flowing skirt. See how the sheer net wings tie to the wrists to flutter realistically as one glides through the air. Adjustable "starred" hatband lends the final magical note. Sizes: 4 to 14 years. (Wand not included.) STATE SIZE. **$7.95**

No. 8 – 35—Wand. . . . . **$ .75**

No. 8 – 65—Ballet—Dainty in material, design and color for the "light fantastic." Consisting of white bloomers with elastic top which are concealed by the dress which has a white rayon bodice and full skirt of layers of stiff white tulle. The head band and skirt have bands of silver besides a number of shiny silver stars. Sizes: 4 to 14 years. STATE SIZE. **$6.40**

No. 8 – 30—Bride with Bouquet—What little girl won't adore being a blushing bride in this loveliest of white costumes? Long crispy Rayon Taffeta dress with ruffly net trim to match the trailing "coroneted" veil that adjusts to any headsize. Pretty lily bouquet with silver tinsel ribbon trim, securely holding the very important ring. Sizes: 6 to 14 years. STATE SIZE. . **$6.95**

No. 8 – 21—Drum Majorette—The vivid red duvetyn jacket is trimmed with gold buttons, braids, and has white epaulets, collar and cuffs. The short full skirt is made of white rayon, trimmed with blue and red. Cape worn over one shoulder is edged with blue. White plush head-dress has gold braid, a red feather plume, white shiny visor and chin strap. Sizes 4-14 years. STATE SIZE. (Baton not included). **$7.95**

No. 7 – 62—Baton—Braided with red and white cord, with tassel. **$1.75**

No. 8 – 25—Drum Major—The impressive Drum Major, and what boy hasn't wished he could be one. Authentically styled, even to the trimmed shako of sleek furry black plush. Suit is of duvetyn, the blouse brilliant red with decorative epaulets, gold braid and brass button trim: the cape to match, the pants blue, striped in red with gold braid. White belt with gold buckle. Sizes 6-14 years. STATE SIZE. (Baton not included). **$7.95**

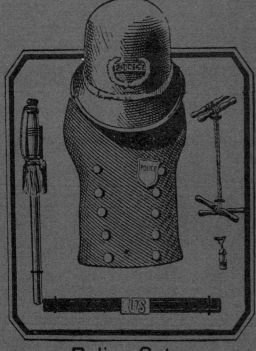

Police Sets.

Strong and durable, mounted on
card, $1.75

Fireman Sets.

With breastplate.................$2.00
Without " $1.50

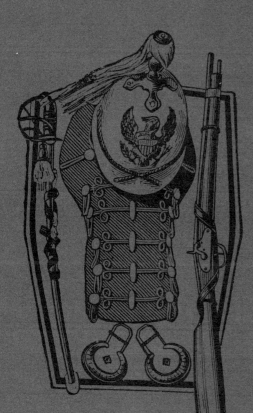

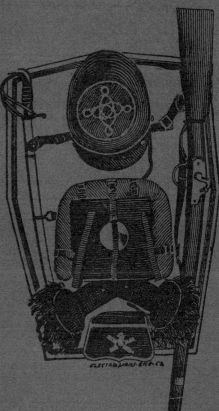

Soldier Equipments on card..................$2.00, $2.50, $3.00, $4.00, $5.00
    " **Caps and Helmets**...............35c., 50c., 65c., 85c., $1.00, $2.00
Metal Armor Sets..........................$3.25, $5.50, $6.50, $10.00
Guns...............25c., 40c., 45c., 50c., 65c., $1.00, $1.25, $1.50, $1.75, $2.50, $3.50
Swords...........25c., 35c., 50c., 75c., $1.00, $1.50, $1.75, $2.50, $4.00, $6.50
Epaulettes......................20c., 25c., 50c., 85c., $1.00 per pair
Cartridge Boxes.................................25c., 75c.
Knapsacks..................................40c., 50c., 60c., 85c.

Gadgets

It is always a challenge to decide how fine gadgets for children should be. The perfect walkie-talkie or the horn that would be acceptable in a symphony are a lot better than play requires. Toy stores have found it difficult to know where to draw the line. At times the gadgets available for children are good enough to fill the requirements of an adult looking for a simple version of a machine.

Cameras are an interesting case in point. By the early 1900s there was photographic equipment available for the person who did not want to bother with all the refinements. The Brownie in the Schwarz catalogue was good enough to take just about anything visible in the viewer. A subject was in focus if it could be seen, and as long as it did not move much it could be photographed. The fixed focus worked for landscapes as well as people. Similarly, biascopes and pocketscopes of the 1920s were fine substitutes for binoculars and telescopes if precision did not matter. Sports and birdwatching were more enjoyable to some without the need for adjusting that the better instruments required.

Changes in communications are easily forgotten. As recently as the 1930s telegraph and telephone sets were still very popular. Learning the Morse code was fun a mere forty years ago but today intercoms obviate the need of the more complex communications systems that were used until after World War II.

Children's musical instruments have not changed much through the years, but phonographs are quite different today from those of the 1930s. It took a much bigger box to house the makings of the earlier phonographs and the contrast between child and adult quality was much more marked. As we can see the more recent sets are a lot smaller because of the technical improvements. These are also responsible for the emergence of the new world of rockets and space instruments.

Magic Lanterns

A Magic Lantern is a most entertaining and instructive article, which will pl[ease]
any boy or girl. Our Lanterns are of superior make and give sharp
and most brilliant pictures. All furnished with slides.
Prices of extra slides given below.

Kinematographs or Moving Picture Machine[s]

[A]ny of these will take the regular Edison Film and can readily be conver[ted]
into an ordinary Magic Lantern.

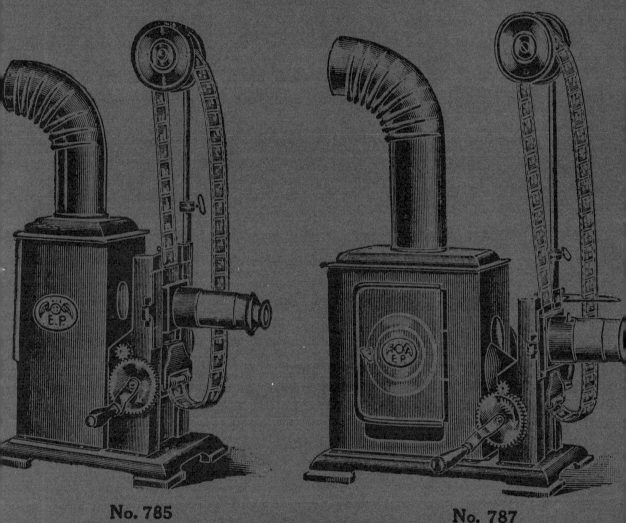

No. 785	**No. 787**
[W]ith 3 colored films and 6 long glass slides, 1¼ inches wide............$2.50	Finer, with 2 colored films, 1 photo film and 12 glass slides, 1½ inches wide......$

LARGER AND FINER APPARATUS...$20.00, $33.00
EXTRA FILMS, about 3 feet long 1.00
    About 10 feet long........$1.50   About 20 feet long........2.00

[AMER]ICANS

[S]everal new styles which we can offer with the assurance of giving the fullest satisfaction.
[Car]d Projectors, they will project not only postal cards but any kind of an opaque picture
[pr]ovide unbounded entertainment and amusement, especially during the long winter evenin[gs]

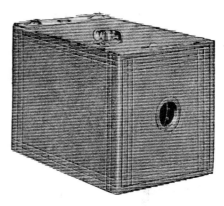

No. 1. BROWNIE CAMERA

Pictures 2¼ x 2¼ in.

No. 1 Brownie Camera, Meniscus Lens.
  Eastman Rotary Shutter.......... **$1.00**
No. 1 Brownie Carrying Case, holds
  Camera and Finder.............. .50
N. C. Film Cartridge, 6 exposures, 2¼x2¼ .15
Brownie Finder, detachable........... .25
No. 1 Brownie Developing and Printing
  Outfit, including paper for 24 prints... .90

No. 2. FOLDING BROWNIE

Pictures 2¼ x 3¼ in.

No. 2 Folding Pocket Brownie, Meniscus
  Lens, Pocket Automatic Shutter.... **$5.00**
No. 2 Folding Pocket Brownie Carrying
  Case............................ .75
N. C. Film Cartridge, 6 exposures,
  2¼ x 3¼........................ .20
Kodak Portrait Attachment........... .50

No. 3. BROWNIE

Pictures 3¼ x 4¼ in.

No. 3 Brownie Camera, Meniscus Achro-
  matic Lens, Eastman Rotary Shutter. **$4.00**
No. 3 Brownie Carrying Case, with shoulder
  strap............................ 1.00
N. C. Film Cartridge, 12 exposures, 3¼x4¼ .70
Ditto, 6 exposures.................... .35
Ditto, "Double Two" Cartridge, 4 expo-
  sures............................ .25
Kodak Portrait Attachment............. .50

1926

FOLDING BROWNIE

No. 2 — Folding Autographic Brownie takes pictures 2¼ x 3¼. Capacity, 6 exposures. Meniscus achromatic lens and kodak ball-bearing shutter, reversible finder **$9.00**

For studying birds and nature, for increasing the pleasure of a motor trip and as an aid in camp, travel and hunting trips, these "Wollensak Scopes" are invaluable.

No. Biascope "A"—Has a six-power magnification, enabling its user to see farther and better with less effort, size 3¼ x 3¾, weight 7½ oz., lever adjustment, black finish, leather case ....each **$5.00**

No. Biascope "B"—Same as "B" in weight and size, but has the improved screw focusing system and pupillary adjustment, black crystallized lacquer finish, genuine leather case ....each **$7.00**

The **Pockescopes** are each supplied with a leather case. They are extremely serviceable, being light and compact and efficient; finished in black crystallized lacquer.

Model	Power	Length (closed)	Price
Pock Jr.	3	2⅝ in.	$1.00
Pock Sr.	6	3¼ in.	2.00

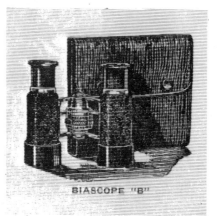

BIASCOPE "B"

POCKESCOPES

$15.00, $20.00, $30.00

1.25, $1.75, $2.50, $3.00, $4.00.

.00.

N.C. Film Cartridge, 12 exposures .70
N.C. Film Cartridge, 6 exposures .35
Kodak Portrait Attachment.......50

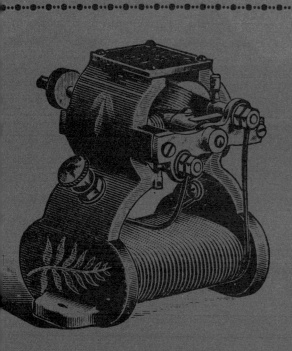

ELECTRIC MOTORS

run small figures, including
battery: $2.50, $3.50 (like
cut) $6.00, $10.00, $12.00
amos..............$6.50, $11.00

ELECTRIC TOP

This is a small motor, upon the ver-
tical axle of which colored discs
are placed. When the motor is
running the discs produce beautiful ever changing color effects.
With battery.................$1.00

ELECTRIC THRILLER

erated by crank. Current
an be moderated according
o speed with which the
rank is turned.........$1.00

TELEPHONES

The "Junior" with metal case, with
4 batteries, wire and instructions.............$8.00 per pair

CHILD'S SYMPHONY

A selection of standard instruments for the Kindergarten Symphony.

No. 735B/8—8 key Cornet	$1.50
No. 374/8—8 key Trombone	1.50
No. 363/8—8 key Saxaphone	1.00
No. 33—Tom-Tom Drums	3.00
No. 6—Triangle	.75
No. 7—Brass Cymbals, pair	1.25
7 inch Tambourine	.75
8 inch Tambourine	1.00
No. K-20—Castanets, pair $0.75, 2 pairs	$1.25

DRUMS

No. 500—8 inch High wood calf	$1.25
No. 500—10 inch Same	2.00
No. 600—11 inch fine low wood	4.00
No. 753/10—10 inch Military Drum	4.50
No. 753/12—12 inch Miliary Drum	5.50
No. 83—14 inch Scout Drum	4.50
No. 83—18 inch same	6.75
No. 800—7½ inch Musical Drum	.85
No. 850—9 inch same	1.75

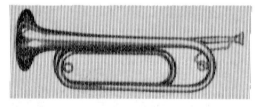

BOY SCOUT BUGLE

This heavy weight brass bugle has a clear, well rounded, tone that carries a long distance; 17" from mouth piece to bell.
..........$5.00

PHONOGRAPH

PHONOGRAPH

Ivory finish, decorated with flowers. Fine quality tone. 17½" x 18½" x 13¾" $15.00
Record Books, each containing 4 children's records, 11 different editions $1.00

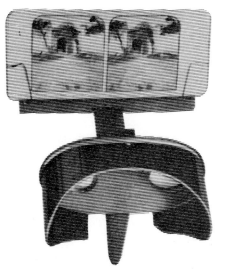

STEREOSCOPE

Made of wood, has strong lenses. Fascinating and instructive amusement for children. With 25 photo views
$4.00

DANDY MORSE LEARNER'S OUTFIT

No. 607—One complete station (sender and receiver) with battery and book of instructions.................$6.00

DUPLEX TELEGRAPH SET

No. 50—Consisting of two transmitting and receiving units with 50 feet of wire and complete instructions for installing. Will operate efficiently up to 1000 feet.

Pair $5.00

Two "C" batteries to operate...............................each 0.50

DIAL PHONE SET (French type)

No. 600—This new set will function well up to 100 ft. with 4-volt battery. It consists of two French type mouth and ear pieces, two dials for calls, wire and battery ready for its installation. All parts finished in crystal black $6.50

DUPLEX TELEPHONE SET

No. 75—Consists of two heavy gauge steel stations, finished in light green duco, with 100 ft. of wire, staples and complete instructions for installing. Will operate efficiently up to 1000 ft. Pair $7.50

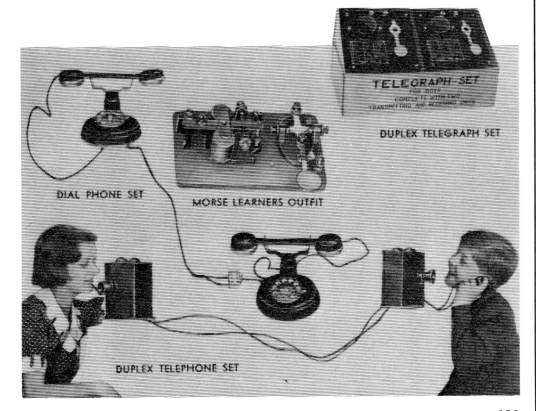

DUPLEX TELEGRAPH SET

DIAL PHONE SET

MORSE LEARNERS OUTFIT

DUPLEX TELEPHONE SET

No. **43 – 32**—**Holmes Theatre De Luxe**—Its chief charm results from movement of characters on stage without any visible mechanical assistance. Characters have stands which protrude through slots in stage floor and can be animated conveniently from below. These slots run in all directions. The 36" high theatre has wood frame covered with green corduroy. Stage has red velvet drop curtain. Electric lights use house current and flood the 12 x 24" stage floor effectively. Included are 6 colored scenic backdrops, 1 sheet with scenic properties to be cut out. Figures not included. For plays see below.
EXCLUSIVE WITH SCHWARZ. **$12.75**

Piano and Bench—New and in a pleasingly modern version. Accurately tuned. Trains the ear and accustoms the child to the true musical scale. Full width key familiarizes little fingers with big piano touch. In maple color.

No. **43 – 48**—18 keys, 22 x 20 x 12". **$11.75**
No. **43 – 47**—37 keys, with half notes that play. Three full octaves, 26 x 23½ x 14½". **$23.75**

Mechanical Swiss Musix Boxes—Cases of polished hardwood, fine key winding mechanism. Unusually rich in tone, depth of tone depending upon number or weight of steel combs.

No. **3 – 21**—Natural wood case, 4¾" long, 2 popular airs. . **$3.75**
No. **3 – 17**—As above but plays 2 Christmas airs. 3.75
No. **3 – 22**—Inlaid brown veneer case 5" long, plays 2 popular airs.
6.75
No. **3 – 18**—As above but plays 2 Christmas airs. 6.75
No. **3 – 73**—Inlaid veneer case, plays 3 popular airs. . . . 10.00
No. **3 – 15**—As above but plays 3 Christmas airs. 10.00

No. 3 – 166—Xylophone—The 12 brass tubes of this musical instrument are lettered and so are the 25 tunes in the instruction book so that musical results are assured rather easily. The longest tube measures 9½'' and the shortest 5''. Held in wooden stand 24'' long and 24'' high. Played with 2 wooden strikers provided.
$3.95

Portable Phonograph—Strong leatherette case 5 x 12 x 15'' with handle. Contains under hinged cover a clear toned phonograph with all parts nickeled. It has velvet covered disc, speed regulator, and needle cup. Convenient record rack in lid.

No. 9 – 85 – 2—BLUE	**$13.50**
No. 9 – 85 – 11—AIRPLANE TAN	13.50
No. 9 – 85 – 3—RED	13.50

No. 9 – 85
Portable Phonograph

No. 2 – 152—Triangle—6'', made of steel with wood knob to give just the right pitch. **$0.75**

No. 2 – 107—Tambourine—7'', with genuine skin head and 6 sets of jingles on wood frame. **$0.75**

No. 2 – 453—Cymbals—7'', made of brass, with strap webbing. Per pair **$1.25**

No. 3 – 108—Drum—This low-built drum has 2 genuine skin heads, 12'' diameter, on wooden shell, with metal hoops and metal adjusting rods. **$3.00**

No. 3 – 65—Typatune—As the name implies it's a musical typewriter. With it one can type a tune by fingering the regulation 32 lettered keyboard, each letter a separate note, giving a 2½ octave range. The Xylophone mechanism is concealed in the back part of the 4 x 11 x 12'' wood case. Tunes of some 20 favorites are written in letters instead of notes in a booklet which is included, so that "Merry Widow", "Comin Thru the Rye", etc., can easily be played. **$10.95**

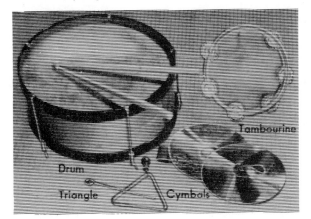

Drum

Triangle Cymbals

Tambourine

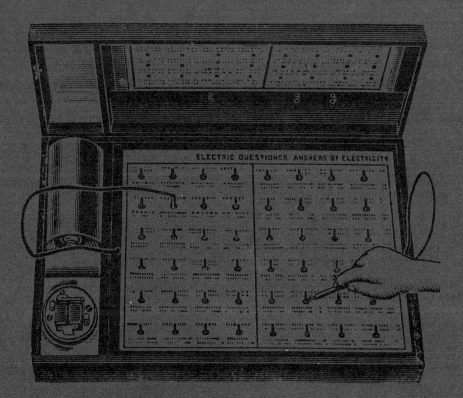

THE ELECTRIC QUESTIONER

48 pins with 24 questions on the left and 24 answers in different rotatio
on the right. When key on the left, is placed on a question, and th
pointer run along the pins on the right, the bell will ring when th
correct answer is found.

Price, with 12 different cards, 24 questions on each side............ $2.5

Set of 12 extra cards .... 50.

SIMPLEX TYPEWRITERS

No. 3. (Like cut) Letter size for capitals, small type and
characters... $3.00

No. 2. Note size for capitals, small type and characters.... 2.00

No. 1. Note size for capitals only............................. 1.00

4-99 GOLDEN SONIC Wt. 7 lbs.........**20.00**
A streamlined all-gold plastic ship on rubber-tired
wheels electrically driven by 4 batteries included.
Throw switch to "on" and Sonic will begin to move. By
blowing on the deep-toned whistle at a few feet
distance the ship will automatically change its course.
Different whistle blows control direction. 20" long.

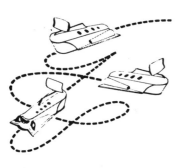

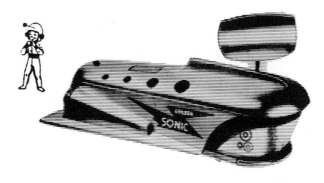

18-153 SPACE ROCKET (Imported) Wt. 2 lbs...**3.95**
Just fasten the original 10" colorful plastic rocket tightly
on the starting and pumping mechanism with the aid
of the bolt. Then pump air into the rocket, hold it in
the desired direction of flight, pull release cord and
off goes the rocket. (Approx. 100 feet.) Partially filled
with water it gives a jet propulsion effect at take-off.
19-8 FIREBIRD "99" DASHBOARD Wt. 4 lbs. ..**7.95**
A very basic, everyday human activity has been
captured in the 13" high-impact plastic Firebird "99".
Completely motorized, the youthful "driver" has only
to switch on the ignition key to be on his imaginary
way. Operating windshield wiper, blinking directional
signals, steering action, and a working horn are
featured, while adjustable rear view mirror, glove
compartment storage area, and working speedometer.
Complete, less batteries.

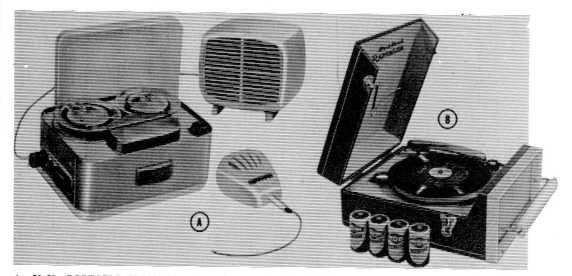

A 31-91 PORTABLE TRANSISTOR TAPE RECORDER....79.95
Parties, celebrations, youngsters speaking their first words are
just a few of the occasions made memorable with this compact,
efficient instrument, whose small size is due to its 4 transistors.
Operating on the four flashlight batteries included, the sensitive
microphone. picks up normal conversational tone and plays it
back with startling clarity. The standard 3" roll tape yields
70 minutes running time. 3" microphone and 4" speaker are
separate units. Tape can be "erased" and used over and
over. Recorder, of grey metal and plastic, is 6¾" x 5" x 3½"
high. Set of batteries lasts 50 hours. (Imp.) Ship. wt. 7 lbs.
B 31-90 TRANSISTOR RADIO-PHONOGRAPH Wt. 7 lbs. **79.95**
A compact, light weight instrument, only 10¾" x 8¾", its
crystal-clear high-fidelity tone is amazing. The lifetime transistors, powered by 4 flashlight batteries, make possible its
small size and light weight. Transistor amplifiers aid in
developing big-voiced volume and distortion-free record reproduction (45 RPM only). One set of batteries yields 6000
record plays or 750 hours of battery play 3" Alnico V speaker,
wood case covered in rust or white simulated ostrich covering,
lucite carrying handle, sapphire needle. Batteries included.

31-219 PORTABLE TRANSISTOR RADIO Wt. 2 lbs.. **65.95**
An amazing product of this electronic age is this 6-transistor
radio that runs on the 4 small flashlight batteries included. The
power and tone are aided by a true fidelity 4" speaker.
Easily carried, it weighs only 28 oz., and is 7½" long, 5" high
and 2½" deep. Batteries last 400 hours, make it extremely
economical to operate. Suntan case of top grain cowhide
has matching handle. Ear plug for private listening included.

5-8 MUSICAL SEWING BOX (Import) Ship. wt. 3 lbs....... **10.95**
A charming version of a very useful gift. When the lid is lifted, a
bright melody is played by the concealed Swiss music box. Gracefully scalloped base is 8 x 12", lined with rayon satin. Underside of
lid holds sewing implements. Made of woven natural rattan.

Banjos $1.00
Flutes, wood . . . . 10c.
Violins . . .25c., 50c., $1.00, $2.00, $2.50, $3.00
Metalophones 50c., $1.00
Mouth Harmonicas, 10c., 15c., 20c., 25c., 35c.,
40c., 50c., 65c., 85c., $1.00
Tambourines . . . . .25c., 50c.
Trombones 25c., 50c., 75c., $1.00, $1.50

ns, plain, wood 25c., 50c., 75c., $1.00, $1.50
fine calf, with fine wood body, high or low shape.
$1.50, $1.75, $2.00, $2.50, $3.50, $5.00
fine calf, with brass or nickel body, $ .00, $2.00,
$2.50, $3.50

Round Metal Horns.

12c., 15c., 20c., 25c., 35c., 50c., $1.00.

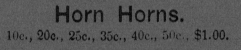

Horn Horns.

10c., 20c., 25c., 35c., 40c., 50c., $1.00.

The Zobo.

A musical instrument requiring
no instruction. Imitates to per-
fection cornet, trombone, tuba, etc.
Plain wood, 10c. . . . . By mail, 12c.
Polished brass, 25c.   "   27c.
. . . . . . large size, fine
quality, $1.00, by
mail, $1.12.

CORNETS.

25c.,	50c.,
$1.25,	$1.50,
2.25,	3.00,
3.50,	5.00.

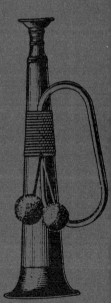

STRAIGHT METAL HORN

5c., 8c., 10c., 20
25c., 35c., 50c., $1.

quare Pianos, good tune, metal notes,

15 keys, $1.00; 17 keys, $1.25; 22 keys, $2.00,

1960

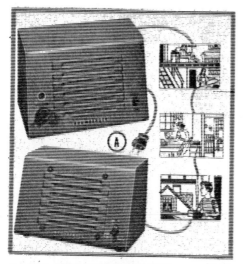

A 4-34 TWO-WAY INTERCOM......29.95
The uses of this excellent intercommunication system are many. By pressing a button, children can speak with "the chief", a "scout" or any other character in their game. Its practical uses are a boon to the lady of the house. Hooked up to playroom, nursery, or basement with "open" switch on, this "electronic baby sitter" enables her to supervise by ear the play of the little ones. Calls can originate at either of the two stations which are housed in modern steel cabinets. Volume controlled Master Station switch has "Talk" and "Listen" positions. Children respond to a call over the intercom—the thrill of speaking to "headquarters" is too much to resist. Simply plug into socket of house current (AC or DC 110 volts). 50 feet of wire included. Ship. wt. 7 lbs.

B 40-36 BEN FRANKLIN PRINT SHOP 24.95
(8 yrs. up)—This printing press is sturdily constructed for long-time use. The youngster with an inclination for journalism never out-grows a gift like this. The fun of printing home-made announcements, programs, or even a "newspaper", is the kind of enjoyment that grows with experience. Includes press, rubber type alphabet, rubber type holder, type tray, tube of printing ink, non-inflammable ink cleaner, type tweezers, screw driver, paper supplies and instruction manual. An educational booklet titled "Adventures In Printing" gives youngsters a good idea of what can be done with the set. Print area is 4" x 2½". Ship. wt. 21 lbs.

C 4-20 DIAL PHONE SET Wt. 5 lbs....**8.00**
(6 yrs. up)—Talking on the telephone holds a fascination for all ages. These excellent life-size instruments, powered by four flashlight batteries, not included, have great play value, and can well be used as interior communications between kitchen and playroom, garage, etc. Just picking up the receiver and dialing rings the phone at the other end. Voice is transmitted loudly and clearly. Phones made of tough black plastic.

D 3-144 CODEMASTER SIGNAL SET 3.95
One of the first steps for the electronically minded youngster is the mastery of code communication. This set of two radio-telegraph signallers in durable plastic makes learning and using the international code fun, featuring communication by light, buzzer, and clicker. 3" x 7" instruments of high-impact plastic are connected by 50 feet of hook-up wire and powered by 4 flashlight batteries (not included, see below). 45 R.P.M. unbreakable Morse Code Instruction record provided along with Western Union blanks for permanent record of messages. Ship. wt. 3 lbs.

A 819-6 ADVANCED ELECTRONICS LAB....**39.95**
(12 yrs. up)—Over 50 fascinating experiments in
electronics. Teaches the principles of electron flow
through construction of transformer, seven types of
radio receivers, two transmitters, public address
system, rain detector, alarm, etc. Parts trays organ-
ize work and serve for storage. Complete with tools
and comprehensive teaching manual.
Ship. wt. 11 lbs.

E 804-51 CODE BROADCASTER **3.95**
Easily built one-transistor circuit to transmit code over any home
radio, up to 300 feet, without wires. Tools included.

**G 804-65 THE YOUNG OPTICIAN AND PHOTOG-
RAPHER** (Import)...............**16.50**
The young optician has at his disposal mirrors,
lenses, glass plates, camera box, film, developing
chemicals, light bulbs, and all parts to perform over
a hundred experiments with light and learn the
secrets of reflection, refraction, magnification, and
photography while making an operating camera,
projector, telescope, microscope, etc. Lots of fun and
very educational. Ship. wt. 3 lbs.

H 803-105 THE YOUNG ELECTRICIAN (Imp.) **12.50**
This basic electrical set contains electrical compon-
ents (coils, wire, lighting parts, etc.) and elements of
magnetism (U magnet, electro-magnet, compass, etc.)
to enable the technically inclined youngster to do
hundreds of fascinating experiments and build practical working devices to illustrate principles he has
learned. An electric motor can be made, also standing lamps, signalling devices, electric buzzer and
bell, burglar alarm, even a working telephone.
Complete with comprehensive instruction booklet
and battery. Ship. wt. 4 lbs.

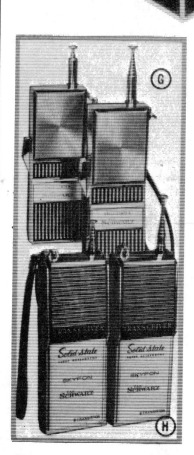

831-533
THE UNIQUE AM/FM RADIO 69.95

A perfect gift for active people. This brand-new AM/FM radio provides listening pleasure indoors and outdoors—even in the most remote area. Play it at home, boat, car, or outdoors on 110 volt AC or batteries included. Highly sensitive circuit design with AGC, AFC and RF amplifier for positive timing and distortion free reception. Unique features include built-in high/low beam flashlight, thermometer, humidity indicator and compass—all actually working. Great for camping and outdoor life. Adjustable strap for easy hand carrying or over the shoulder. 10¼"x8"x3". (Import) Ship. wt. 5 lbs.

F 831-503 SOLID STATE WIRELESS INTERCOM 34.50

Merely plug the two smart-looking transistorized 6¼"x 4¼"x1¾" sending-receiving stations into any convenient 110 volt household current outlet and play in their desired locations (upstairs, downstairs, garage, etc.) within the operating range of 100 to 1500 feet. No extra wiring needed. Conversations are loud and clear. With volume control, pilot light, and call button. Excellent "baby sitter". (Import) Ship. wt. 5 lbs.

G 831-510 JR. WALKIE-TALKIE SET 29.95

Two complete transistorized Walkie-Talkie units for local chatter. Press switch to talk, release to listen, as conversations come over loud and clear up to ¼ mile. Children will enjoy this latest electronic aid to Cops and Robbers, Hide and Go Seek, etc. 2¼"x6¾", encased in very durable combination die-cast and plastic housing, with carry strap and batteries. (Import) Ship. wt. 4 lbs.

H 831-561 WALKIE-TALKIE SET
(Set of 2) 39.95

(Import)—New 8-transistor Walkie-Talkie equipped with 2 crystals for very clear transmission through loudspeaker with a range of over one mile on land and 2½ miles on water. Sturdy 2½"x7" all metal die-cast cabinet with chrome-trimmed speaker, built-in 39" telescopic antenna, volume control, push-to-talk switch, and a handy new feature—a push button "Call Buzzer" on each unit to command instant attention. With carry strap, battery, instructions. Ship. wt. 4 lbs.

TOOL CABINETS

Wooden, with good quality tools........ ...... $8.00

10.00, 15.00, 20.00, 30.00

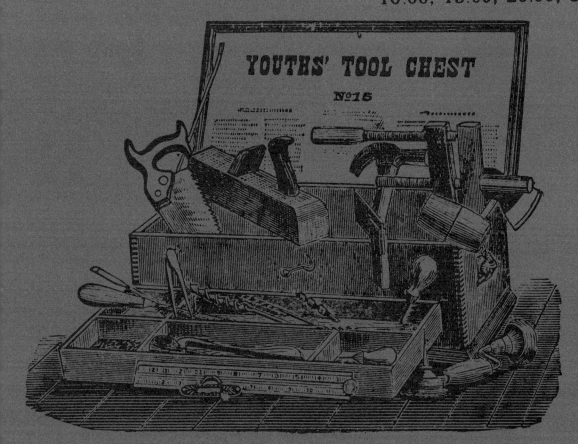

TOOL CHESTS

In mahogany stained box, fair quality tools, for children
75c., $1.25, $1.75, $2.50, $3.00, $4.00
Better quality tools, for youths $7.50, $12.00, $18.00

ELECTRIC TELEGRAPH OUTFIT

Consisting of 1 Station, Battery and Book of Instructions $2.50
Miniature Outfit...................................... 1.50